Darling Ha~

With m... ... ...
embark on married life!

Happy cooking!

Ruthie.
———
X

9/4/10.

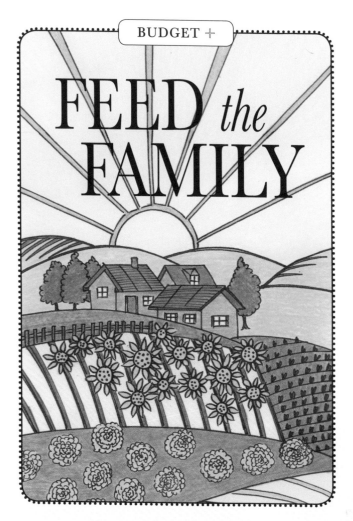

BUDGET +

FEED *the* FAMILY

more than 80 satisfying recipes

MURDOCH BOOKS

Published in 2010 by Murdoch Books Pty Limited

Murdoch Books Australia
Pier 8/9
23 Hickson Road
Millers Point NSW 2000
Phone: +61 (0) 2 8220 2000
Fax: +61 (0) 2 8220 2558
www.murdochbooks.com.au

Murdoch Books UK Limited
Erico House, 6th Floor
93–99 Upper Richmond Road
Putney, London SW15 2TG
Phone: +44 (0) 20 8785 5995
Fax: +44 (0) 20 8785 5985
www.murdochbooks.co.uk

Chief Executive: Juliet Rogers
Publishing Director: Kay Scarlett
Publisher: Lynn Lewis
Concept, Design and Illustrations: Heather Menzies
Editor: Margaret Malone
Production: Alexandra Gonzalez
Index: Jo Rudd

National Library of Australia Cataloguing-in-Publication Data

Title: Feed the Family.
ISBN: 9781741966756 (hbk.)
Series: Budget +. Notes: Includes index.
Subjects: Home economics.
Dewey Number: 640.994

A catalogue record for this book is available from the British Library.

PRINTED IN CHINA. Printed in 2009.

CONTENTS

INTRODUCTION 5

FROM THE FIELD 6

FROM THE PASTURE & FARMYARD...26

FROM THE STREAM & OCEAN 58

FROM THE KITCHEN GARDEN 70

FROM THE DAIRY 94

INDEX 108

Tried and trusted recipes are what everyone is looking for these days. We want good food, familiar ingredients, nothing complicated…the kinds of things we want to eat every day because they don't just satisfy our hunger, they make us feel good.

So, we've put together a selection of recipes that are not too lengthy and not too complicated, either. They're ideal, in fact, for busy people who are a bit short on time and energy at the end of a hard day's work.

We've grouped the recipes according to where the main ingredients would have come from…the stream, the paddock, the kitchen garden or dairy. There's nothing too obscure or overly expensive (though we've allowed for the occasional treat, of course). You'll see that there's plenty of fresh produce included, such as chicken, eggs, vegetables and fish, and plenty of kitchen standbys, too, from the fridge, freezer or pantry. Mostly, you'll probably have them there already. Some recipes have the odd ingredient that you might have to search for but most can be put together from the local supermarket or high street shops. A weekend trip to the farmer's market will help, too, if you do a bit of planning ahead.

Some dishes require a little time to prepare and have a short cooking time; others can be thrown together and then left to cook for a while. Most of the recipes serve four people but should you have more mouths to feed, you can add to them without much ado. That's it, really!

FROM THE FIELD

FLOUR 8

NOODLES 16

RICE 20

SPAGHETTI PUTTANESCA

400 G (14 OZ) SPAGHETTI

1 TABLESPOON OLIVE OIL

1 ONION, FINELY CHOPPED

2 GARLIC CLOVES, FINELY SLICED

1 SMALL RED CHILLI, CORED, SEEDED AND SLICED

4 ANCHOVY FILLETS, FINELY CHOPPED

400 G (14 OZ) TINNED CHOPPED TOMATOES

1 TABLESPOON FINELY CHOPPED OREGANO

12 BLACK OLIVES, HALVED AND PITTED

2 TABLESPOONS BABY CAPERS

1 HANDFUL BASIL LEAVES

Cook the spaghetti in a large saucepan of boiling salted water until just tender (al dente), stirring once or twice to make sure the strands are not sticking together. The cooking time will vary depending on the brand of spaghetti. Check the pasta occasionally as it cooks because the time given on packets is only a guide and you don't want to overcook it.

Heat the olive oil in a large saucepan and add the onion, garlic and chilli. Gently fry everything for about 6 minutes, or until the onion is soft, then add the anchovies and cook for another minute. Add the tomato, oregano, olive halves and capers and bring to the boil. Reduce the heat, season with salt and pepper, and leave the sauce to simmer for 2 minutes.

Drain the spaghetti and add it to the sauce. Toss both together well so that the pasta is coated in sauce. Scatter the basil over the top and serve.

SPAGHETTI CARBONARA

1 TABLESPOON OLIVE OIL
200 G (7 OZ) PANCETTA, CUBED
125 ML (4 FL OZ/$^1/_2$ CUP) THICK (DOUBLE/HEAVY) CREAM
4 EGG YOLKS
400 G (14 OZ) SPAGHETTI
6 TABLESPOONS GRATED PARMESAN CHEESE

Heat the olive oil in a saucepan and cook the pancetta, stirring frequently, until it is light brown and crisp. Tip the pancetta into a sieve to strain off any excess oil.

Combine the cream and egg yolks in a bowl. When the pancetta has cooled, add it to the egg mixture.

Cook the spaghetti in a large saucepan of boiling salted water until just tender (al dente), stirring once or twice to make sure the strands are not sticking together. The cooking time will vary depending on the brand of spaghetti. Check the pasta occasionally as it cooks because the time given on packets is only a guide and you don't want to overcook it. Drain the spaghetti and reserve a small cup of the cooking water.

Return the spaghetti to the saucepan and place over a low heat. Add the egg mixture and 3 tablespoons of parmesan, then quickly take the pan off the heat, otherwise the egg will scramble. Season with salt and pepper and combine everything quickly. If the sauce is too thick and the pasta is stuck together, add a little reserved cooking water. The spaghetti should look as if it has a fine coating of egg and cream all over it.

Serve the spaghetti in warm bowls with the remaining parmesan sprinkled over the top.

SPINACH AND RICOTTA RAVIOLI

1 TABLESPOON OLIVE OIL
1 SMALL RED ONION, FINELY CHOPPED
2 GARLIC CLOVES, CRUSHED
200 G (7 OZ) BABY SPINACH LEAVES, COARSELY CHOPPED
250 G (9 OZ/1 CUP) FRESH RICOTTA
2 EGG YOLKS, BEATEN
2 TABLESPOONS GRATED PARMESAN CHEESE
FRESHLY GRATED NUTMEG
ABOUT 48 WON TON WRAPPERS
60 G (2 OZ) BUTTER
2 TABLESPOONS SAGE LEAVES

Heat the oil in a frying pan, add the onion and garlic and fry over low heat for a few minutes until the onion goes soft and translucent. Add the spinach; stir it around until it wilts. If there is any liquid left in the pan, turn up the heat and pull spinach to one side so the liquid can evaporate.

Stir spinach mixture into the ricotta, along with the egg yolks, parmesan, some nutmeg and some salt and pepper.

Brush a little water around the edge of a won ton wrapper and put a teaspoon of filling in the centre. Fold the wrapper over to make a half moon shape and press the edges firmly together. Place on a tea towel (dish towel) laid out on your work surface and repeat with remaining wrappers and filling.

Bring a large saucepan of water to the boil and cook the ravioli for a few minutes. They will float to the surface when ready. Scoop them out carefully with a slotted spoon and drain in a colander. Melt the butter in a small pan, add sage and sizzle for a few minutes until the butter browns slightly. Put the ravioli in bowls and pour the butter and sage over them.

MINESTRONE WITH PESTO

1 TABLESPOON OLIVE OIL

1 ONION, FINELY CHOPPED

2 GARLIC CLOVES, FINELY CHOPPED

2 TABLESPOONS FINELY CHOPPED FLAT-LEAF (ITALIAN) PARSLEY

100 G (3½ OZ) PANCETTA, CUBED

1 CELERY STALK, HALVED, THEN DICED

1 CARROT, DICED

2 TEASPOONS TOMATO PASTE (CONCENTRATED PURÉE)

400 G (14 OZ) TINNED CHOPPED TOMATOES

1.5 LITRES (52 FL OZ/6 CUPS) CHICKEN OR VEGETABLE STOCK

2 ZUCCHINI (COURGETTES), DICED

40 G (1½ OZ/¼ CUP) PEAS

12 RUNNER BEANS, CUT INTO SHORT LENGTHS

2 HANDFULS FINELY SHREDDED SAVOY CABBAGE

4 TABLESPOONS DITALINI OR OTHER SMALL PASTA

300 G (10½ OZ) TINNED BORLOTTI OR CANNELLINI BEANS

4 TABLESPOONS READY-MADE PESTO

Melt the oil in a large saucepan and add the onion, garlic, parsley and pancetta. Cook over a very low heat, stirring the mixture once or twice, for about 10 minutes, or until the onion is soft and golden.

Add the celery and carrot and cook them for 5 minutes. Stir in the tomato paste and tomato with plenty of pepper. Add stock and bring slowly to the boil. Cover and leave to simmer for 30 minutes, stirring once or twice.

Taste for seasoning and adjust if necessary. Add the zucchini, peas, runner beans, cabbage, ditalini and drained and rinsed borlotti beans. Simmer for a couple of minutes until the pasta is just tender (al dente). Serve with pesto spooned into the middle of each bowl of minestrone.

HAM, ARTICHOKE AND SPINACH LASAGNE

40 G (1$^1/_2$ OZ) BUTTER

2 TABLESPOONS PLAIN (ALL-PURPOSE) FLOUR

2 PINCHES FRESHLY GRATED NUTMEG

625 ML (21$^1/_2$ FL OZ/2$^1/_2$ CUPS) MILK

1 BAY LEAF

1 TABLESPOON OLIVE OIL

2 GARLIC CLOVES, CRUSHED

200 G (7 OZ) BABY SPINACH LEAVES

6 LARGE FRESH LASAGNE SHEETS OR READY-COOK DRY PASTA SHEETS

8 SLICES HAM

6 ARTICHOKE HEARTS, SLICED

4 TABLESPOONS GRATED PARMESAN CHEESE

Preheat the oven to 180°C (350°F/Gas 4). Heat the butter in a small saucepan over low heat. Stir in the flour and nutmeg and cook, stirring continuously, for 1 minute. Take the pan off the heat and gradually stir in the milk. Add the bay leaf and put the pan back on the heat. Stirring the mixture often so it doesn't go lumpy, simmer until the béchamel sauce is the consistency of thick cream. Keep cooking it for a minute or two to make sure the flour cooks properly – if you don't, the sauce will taste of uncooked flour. Season with salt and pepper. Discard the bay leaf.

Heat the olive oil in a frying pan, add the garlic and let it sizzle for a minute before adding the spinach and stirring it around until it wilts. Cook the lasagne sheets in a large saucepan of boiling, salted water for about 3 minutes, then drain well. Trim the lasagne sheets to fit a 30 cm (12 inch) square ovenproof dish.

Put a ladleful of the sauce onto the bottom of the dish and lay a sheet of lasagne on top. Put four slices of ham, half of the spinach and half of the artichokes on top and drizzle with a little more sauce. Top with another lasagne sheet, then another layer of filling. Place the final lasagne sheet on top and pour the rest of the sauce over it. Scatter the parmesan over the top.

Put the lasagne in the oven and turn the oven down to 170°C (325°F/ Gas 3). Put a baking tray on the bottom shelf of the oven to catch any sauce if the lasagne bubbles over. Cook lasagne for 30 minutes, then let it sit for 5 minutes before serving. Serve with a mixture of salad leaves.

COOK'S TIP There are few ingredients more instantly connected with Italian cooking than pasta, in all its delicious forms. This lasagne should have lots of filling and a good layer of béchamel sauce on top. When you cook it, put a baking tray on the bottom shelf of the oven to catch any sauce if the lasagne bubbles over. A close second to pasta in the Italian cooking lexicon, is parmesan cheese. This hard cow's milk cheese should be bought in a chunk and grated only as needed, rather than purchased ready-grated. Parmigiano Reggiano is widely regarded as the best variety.

PIZZA MARGHERITA

1 PACKET PIZZA BASE MIX (OR A READY-MADE BASE)
4 VERY RIPE ROMA (PLUM) TOMATOES
12 BASIL LEAVES
2 GARLIC CLOVES, CRUSHED
1 TABLESPOON PASSATA (PURÉED TOMATOES)
4 TABLESPOONS OLIVE OIL
200 G (7 OZ) MOZZARELLA CHEESE BALL, CHOPPED

If you are using a packet mix, make up the pizza base following the instructions on the packet and leave it to prove. Heat the oven to as high as it will go – pizzas should cook as quickly as possible at a high heat.

Take the cores, seeds and juice out of the tomatoes, then chop the flesh roughly and purée it in a food processor with 4 basil leaves. (If you don't have a food processor, chop the tomato flesh and basil very finely and stir them together.) Stir in the garlic, passata and 2 tablespoons of olive oil and season well.

Roll out the pizza base to a 30 cm (12 inch) circle and put it on an oiled baking try – if it shrinks when you move it, just stretch it out again. Drizzle it with a little of the olive oil. Spoon the tomato sauce over the base, spreading it up to the rim. Scatter the mozzarella over the top and drizzle with a little more olive oil.

Cook the pizza for 10–12 minutes (this will depend on how hot your oven is), or until the base is light brown and crisp and the topping is cooked. Before serving, drizzle with a little more oil and scatter the remaining basil on top. Cut into wedges to serve. Makes 1 large pizza

SOY AND LINSEED LOAF

110 G (3³/₄ OZ/¹/₂ CUP) PEARL BARLEY
2 TEASPOONS DRIED YEAST
1 TEASPOON CASTER (SUPERFINE) SUGAR
1 TABLESPOON LINSEEDS (FLAX SEEDS)
2 TABLESPOONS SOY FLOUR
2 TABLESPOONS GLUTEN FLOUR
150 G (5¹/₂ OZ/1 CUP) WHOLEMEAL (WHOLE-WHEAT) STRONG FLOUR
310 G (11 OZ/2¹/₂ CUPS) WHITE STRONG FLOUR
2 TABLESPOONS OLIVE OIL

Brush a 10 x 26 cm (4 x 10¹/₂ inch) bread tin with oil. Put the barley
in a pan with 500 ml (17 fl oz/2 cups) water, and boil for 20 minutes.
Drain. Put the yeast, sugar and 150 ml (5 fl oz) warm water in a bowl
and mix. Leave in a draught-free place for 10 minutes, or until bubbles
appear. If your yeast doesn't foam, it is dead, and you'll need to start again.

Put the barley, linseeds, soy, gluten and wholemeal flour, 250 g (9 oz/
2 cups) of the white flour and 1 teaspoon salt in a bowl. Make a well in
the centre and add the yeast mixture, oil and 150 ml (5 fl oz) warm water.
Mix to a soft dough. Turn onto a floured surface and knead for 10 minutes.
Incorporate enough flour until the dough is no longer sticky.

Place in an oiled bowl and brush the dough with oil. Cover with plastic
wrap and leave in a warm, draught-free place for 45 minutes, or until
doubled in size. Punch down and knead for 2–3 minutes. Pat the dough
into a 20 x 24 cm (8 x 9¹/₂ inch) rectangle. Roll up from the long side and
place, seam side down, in the bread tin. Cover with plastic wrap and set
aside for 1 hour. Preheat the oven to 200°C (400°F/Gas 6).

Brush dough with water and make two slits on top. Bake for 30 minutes.
Remove from the tin and cool on a wire rack. Makes 1 loaf

RAMEN NOODLE SOUP WITH CHAR SIU

300 G (10½ OZ) DRIED THIN RAMEN EGG NOODLES, ABOUT 8 NESTS
1 LITRE (35 FL OZ/4 CUPS) CHICKEN STOCK
4 SPRING ONIONS (SCALLIONS), SHREDDED
4 TABLESPOONS SOY SAUCE
400 G (14 OZ) CHAR SIU, ABOUT 10 CM (4 INCHES) LONG
2 SMALL BOK CHOY (PAK CHOY), ROUGHLY CHOPPED
SESAME OIL, FOR DRIZZLING

Cook the noodles in a large saucepan of boiling salted water for about 4 minutes, or until they are just cooked, stirring once or twice to make sure they are not stuck together. The cooking time will vary depending on the brand of noodles.

Bring the chicken stock to the boil in a saucepan, then add the spring onion and soy sauce. Taste the stock to see if it has enough flavour and, if not, add a bit more soy sauce – don't overdo it, though, as the soup's base should be quite mild in flavour. Turn the heat down to a simmer. Cut the char siu into bite-sized shreds or slices (small enough to pick up and eat with chopsticks).

Drain the noodles and divide them between two bowls. Add the bok choy to the chicken stock, stir it in, then divide the stock and vegetables among the four bowls. Arrange the char siu on top, then drizzle a little sesame oil onto each – sesame oil has a very strong flavour, so you will only need a couple of drops for each bowl.

RICE NOODLES WITH BEEF AND BLACK BEANS

300 G (10¹/₂ OZ) RUMP STEAK

2 GARLIC CLOVES, CRUSHED

3 TABLESPOONS OYSTER SAUCE

2 TEASPOONS SUGAR

2 TABLESPOONS SOY SAUCE

125 ML (4 FL OZ/¹/₂ CUP) BLACK BEAN SAUCE

2 TEASPOONS CORNFLOUR (CORNSTARCH)

1 TEASPOON SESAME OIL

1.2 KG (2 LB 12 OZ) FRESH OR 600 G (1 LB 5 OZ) DRIED FLAT RICE NOODLES

1 TABLESPOON OIL

1 LARGE RED CAPSICUM (PEPPER), SHREDDED

1 SMALL GREEN CAPSICUM (PEPPER), SHREDDED

A LARGE HANDFUL CORIANDER (CILANTRO) LEAVES

Cut the steak across the grain into thin slices and put it in a bowl with the garlic, oyster sauce, sugar, soy sauce, black bean sauce, cornflour and sesame oil. Combine everything, making sure the slices are all well coated.

If you are using dried rice noodles, soak them in boiling water for about 10 minutes, or until opaque and soft. If the noodles are particularly dry, they may need a little longer. Drain the noodles.

Heat the oil in a wok or frying pan and, when hot, add the red and green capsicum. Stir-fry for a minute or two until starting to soften, then add the meat mixture and cook for a minute. Add the noodles and toss everything together well. Keep cooking until the meat is cooked through and everything is hot, then toss in the coriander leaves and stir once before turning off the heat. Serve straight away.

THAI-STYLE CHICKEN WITH GLASS NOODLES

4 TABLESPOONS COCONUT CREAM
1 TABLESPOON FISH SAUCE
1 TABLESPOON PALM SUGAR (JAGGERY), GRATED
2 BONELESS, SKINLESS CHICKEN BREASTS, SHREDDED
120 G ($4^1/_4$ OZ) GLASS NOODLES
2 LEMON GRASS STEMS
4 MAKRUT (KAFFIR LIME) LEAVES
1 RED ONION, FINELY CHOPPED
1 LARGE HANDFUL CORIANDER (CILANTRO) LEAVES, CHOPPED
1 LARGE HANDFUL MINT LEAVES, CHOPPED
1 LARGE RED CHILLI, SEEDED AND SLICED
2–3 GREEN BIRD'S EYE CHILLIES, SEEDED AND FINELY SLICED
2 TABLESPOONS CHOPPED ROASTED PEANUTS
2 LIMES, CUT IN HALVES OR QUARTERS

Mix the coconut cream in a small saucepan or a wok with the fish sauce and palm sugar and bring to the boil, then add the chicken and simmer until the chicken is cooked through. This should only take a minute or two if you stir it a couple of times. Leave the chicken to cool in the sauce. Soak the noodles in boiling water for a minute or two. Drain them, then, using a pair of scissors, cut them into shorter lengths.

Peel the lemon grass until you reach the first purplish ring, then trim off the root. Make two or three cuts down the bulb-like root, finely slice across it until it starts to get harder, then throw the hard top piece away. Pull the stems out of the lime leaves by folding the leaves in half, with the shiny side inwards, and pulling down on the stalk. Roll up the leaves tightly, then very finely slice them across.

Put all the ingredients, except the lime, in a bowl with the noodles and chicken, with its sauce, and toss everything together. Now squeeze the

lime pieces over the dish and toss again. (You can adjust the flavouring
at the table, if you like, by putting the lime pieces, sugar, chopped chillies
and fish on the table as condiments.)

COOK'S TIP This summery noodle dish is inspired by the Thai practice
of combining flavourings to produce a hot, sweet, sour and salty flavour –
often all at once. One key ingredient in this dish is palm sugar, or jaggery,
a dark unrefined sugar obtained from the sap of sugar palm trees. It is
widely used in Southeast Asian cooking, not only in sweet dishes but to
balance the flavours in savoury ones. Buy palm sugar in blocks or jars and
shave the sugar off the block with a sharp knife or grate it. This salad does
take a little time to prepare as it involves a lot of chopping, but is then
very quick to put together.

SALMON KEDGEREE

1 LITRE (35 FL OZ/4 CUPS) FISH OR VEGETABLE STOCK
400 G (14 OZ) SALMON FILLET, ABOUT 2 THICK 8 CM (3 INCH) PIECES
3 TABLESPOONS BUTTER
1 TABLESPOON OIL
1 LARGE ONION, CHOPPED
2 TEASPOONS MADRAS CURRY PASTE
200 G (7 OZ) LONG-GRAIN RICE
2 HARD-BOILED EGGS, CUT INTO WEDGES
4 TABLESPOONS CHOPPED FLAT-LEAF (ITALIAN) PARSLEY
4 TABLESPOONS CREAM
LEMON WEDGES

Put the stock in a frying pan and bring it to the boil. Put the salmon fillet in the stock, put a lid on the frying pan and turn the heat down to a simmer. Cook the salmon for 3 minutes, by which time it should feel firm when pressed and look opaque. Lift it out of the stock and flake it into large pieces by pulling it apart gently with your hands.

Melt 2 tablespoons of the butter in a frying pan with the oil, add the onion and gently cook it over low heat until the onion softens. Stir in the curry paste, then add the rice and mix everything together until it is all coated. Add the fish stock, mix it in, then bring the mixture to the boil.

Simmer the rice with the lid on over a very low heat for about 8 minutes, then add the salmon and cook, covered, for another 5 minutes, by which time all the liquid should be absorbed. If the rice is too dry and not yet cooked, add a splash of boiling water and keep cooking for a minute or two.

Stir in the remaining butter, the egg, parsley and cream (leave the cream out if you like – the kedgeree just won't be as rich) and serve with the lemon to squeeze over.

SPECIAL FRIED RICE WITH PRAWNS

200 G (7 OZ/1 CUP) LONG-GRAIN RICE
3 EGGS
2 SPRING ONIONS (SCALLION), CHOPPED
4 TABLESPOONS PEAS
1 TABLESPOON OIL
10 ASPARAGUS SPEARS, CUT INTO 2.5 CM (1 INCH) LENGTHS
20 RAW PRAWNS (SHRIMP), PEELED, DEVEINED AND HALVED LENGTHWAYS
1 OR 2 TEASPOONS SESAME OIL

Cook the rice in simmering water for 12 minutes, or until it is cooked, then drain. Lightly beat the eggs in a bowl with the spring onion and a pinch of salt.

Cook the peas in simmering water for 3 to 4 minutes for fresh, or about 1 minute for frozen. Drain and add to the rice.

Heat a wok over high heat, add the oil and heat until very hot. Add the asparagus and prawns and cook, stirring continuously, until the prawns are pink. Reduce the heat, add the egg and lightly scramble. Before the egg is set too hard, add the rice and peas and increase the heat. Stir to separate the rice and peas and increase the heat. Stir again to separate the rice grains and break the egg into small bits. Season with salt and stir in 1 teaspoon sesame oil. Taste and add more sesame oil, if required.

BUTTERNUT AND FETA RISOTTO

2 TABLESPOONS OLIVE OIL

6 GARLIC CLOVES, UNPEELED

1 THYME SPRIG

1 SMALL BUTTERNUT PUMPKIN (SQUASH), PEELED AND CUBED

1 LITRE (35 FL OZ/4 CUPS) CHICKEN OR VEGETABLE STOCK

20 G ($^3/_4$ OZ) BUTTER

1 ONION, FINELY CHOPPED

300 G ($10^1/_2$ OZ/$1^1/_3$ CUPS) RISOTTO RICE

125 ML (4 FL OZ/$^1/_2$ CUP) DRY WHITE WINE

4 TABLESPOONS FINELY CHOPPED FLAT-LEAF (ITALIAN) PARSLEY

80 G ($2^3/_4$ OZ) FETA CHEESE, CRUMBLED

FRESHLY GRATED PARMESAN CHEESE

Preheat the oven to 200°C (400°F/Gas 6). Put the olive oil in a roasting tin with the garlic, thyme and butternut pumpkin. Coat everything in the oil and season well. Roast in the oven for about 25 minutes, turning everything over once. Take the garlic out of its papery skin but leave it whole. Throw away the thyme.

Heat the stock in a saucepan until it is simmering, then leave it over low heat. Melt the butter in a large, deep, heavy-based frying pan, then gently cook the onion until it is soft, but not browned. Add the rice, reduce the heat to low and stir well to coat all the grains of rice in the butter.

Add the wine to the rice, increase the heat to medium and cook, stirring, until all the liquid has been absorbed. Add the hot stock, a couple of ladles at a time, stirring continuously so that the rice cooks evenly and releases some of its starch. This is what gives risotto a creamy consistency.

Once all the stock has been added to the rice, taste the rice to see if it is just tender (al dente). It is impossible to gauge the exact amount of liquid you will need as every risotto will be a little different. If the rice is not yet cooked and you have run out of stock, use water. Stop cooking the rice as soon as it is soft but still has a little texture or bite in the middle of the grain. Taste the risotto and add seasoning if it needs it. Stir in the butternut pumpkin, garlic, parsley and feta, squashing the vegetables slightly as you stir. Serve with grated parmesan.

COOK'S TIP Risotto is an ideal dish to cook for someone else, preferably someone you can talk to as you cook. Arborio, carnaroli or vialone nano are relatively common varieties of risotto rice. You can use any one of them, but cooking times will vary. When cooking, use a deep frying pan with a heavy base that distributes the heat evenly and prevents the rice burning. Keep the stock hot so that you don't cool the risotto down every time you add a little, and stir constantly (don't let your dinner companion distract you). This way, the rice will cook evenly and you will get that lovely, creamy texture you are after.

PULAO WITH FRIED ONIONS AND SPICED CHICKEN

1 LITRE (35 FL OZ/4 CUPS) CHICKEN STOCK

3 TABLESPOONS OIL

4 CARDAMOM PODS

7 CM (3 INCH) PIECE CINNAMON STICK

3 CLOVES

5 BLACK PEPPERCORNS

270 G (9½ OZ/1⅓ CUPS) BASMATI RICE

2 HANDFULS CORIANDER (CILANTRO) LEAVES

1 LARGE ONION, FINELY SLICED

2 TEASPOONS CURRY PASTE (ANY TYPE)

1 TABLESPOON TOMATO PASTE (CONCENTRATED PURÉE)

2 TABLESPOONS PLAIN YOGHURT

400 G (14 OZ) BONELESS, SKINLESS CHICKEN BREASTS, CUT INTO STRIPS

THICK PLAIN YOGHURT, TO SERVE

MANGO CHUTNEY, TO SERVE

Heat the stock in a saucepan until it is simmering. Heat 1 tablespoon of the oil over medium heat in a large heavy-based saucepan. Add the cardamom pods, cinnamon stick, cloves and peppercorns and fry for 1 minute. Reduce heat to low, add rice and stir constantly for 1 minute. Add the heated stock and some salt to the rice and quickly bring mixture to the boil. Cover the saucepan and simmer the rice over a low heat for 15 minutes. Leave the rice to stand for 10 minutes. Stir in the coriander.

Heat a tablespoon of the oil in a frying pan and fry the onion until it is very soft. Increase the heat and keep frying until the onion turns dark brown. Drain the onion on paper towels, then add it to the rice.

Mix the curry paste, tomato paste and yoghurt together, then mix the paste thoroughly with the chicken strips.

Heat the remaining oil in a frying pan. Cook the chicken for 4 minutes over high heat until almost black in patches. Serve the rice with the chicken strips, yoghurt and mango chutney.

COOK'S TIP A pulao is a spiced rice dish that can be eaten with pretty much anything. Its versatility is its strength, which accounts for its enduring popularity. In the Middle East and Turkey you will find pilaffs, in Russia pilavs, and in the deep south of America purloos. These simple rice dishes go well with curries and roast meat, while in this dish, you can easily transform it into a vegetarian meal by omitting the chicken and adding some steamed or stir-fried vegetables. Similarly, other grains can be used as the base – burghul, barley, buckwheat, quinoa or even lentils.

FROM THE
PASTURE & FARMYARD

BEEF 28

LAMB 36

PORK 43

CHICKEN 51

HAMBURGERS WITH FRESH CORN RELISH

500 G (1 LB 2 OZ) MINCED (GROUND) BEEF

1 GARLIC CLOVE, CRUSHED

1 LARGE ONION, VERY FINELY CHOPPED

2 TABLESPOONS FINELY CHOPPED FLAT-LEAF (ITALIAN) PARSLEY

1 TABLESPOON TOMATO SAUCE (KETCHUP)

A FEW DROPS WORCESTERSHIRE SAUCE

2 COBS OF CORN

2 TOMATOES, FINELY CHOPPED

1 TABLESPOON SWEET CHILLI SAUCE

1 LARGE HANDFUL CORIANDER (CILANTRO) LEAVES

LIME JUICE

1 TABLESPOON OIL

4 SOFT HAMBURGER ROLLS

BABY COS (ROMAINE)

Turn on the grill (broiler). Put the beef in a bowl with the garlic, half of the onion, the parsley and the tomato and worcestershire sauces. Season and mix well, then leave to marinate while you make the relish.

Grill (broil) the corn cob until it is slightly blackened and cooked. Slice off the kernels and mix them with the tomato, chilli sauce, coriander and remaining onion. Add the lime juice and salt and pepper, to taste.

Form the beef mixture into 4 large patties and flatten them out to the size of the buns (bear in mind that they will shrink as they cook). Heat the oil in a frying pan and fry the beef patties for between 3 and 5 minutes on each side, depending on how well cooked you like them. While they are cooking, toast the buns.

Lay a lettuce leaf or two on each bun bottom, add some relish and top with a hamburger and the bun top. Serve any extra relish on the side.

CHUNKY CHILLI CON CARNE

165 g (6 oz) black beans or kidney beans

2 tablespoons oil

1 large red onion, finely chopped

2 garlic cloves, crushed

a large handful coriander (cilantro) leaves, finely chopped

1 or 2 chillies, seeded and finely chopped

1 kg (2 lb 4 oz) chuck steak, cut into cubes

400 g (14 oz) tinned chopped tomatoes

1 tablespoon tomato paste (concentrated purée)

375 ml (13 fl oz/1 1/2 cups) beef stock

1 large red capsicum (pepper), diced

2 ripe tomatoes, chopped

1 avocado, diced

1 lime, juiced

4 tablespoons sour cream

Soak the beans in cold water overnight. The next day, drain and rinse them well. Heat half of the oil in a heatproof casserole and cook three-quarters of the onion, the garlic, half of the coriander, and the chilli, for 5 minutes.

Turn up the heat, push the onion to one side and add the remaining oil. Add the steak and cook for 1–2 minutes. Add the beans, tomato, tomato paste and stock and stir everything together well. Bring the mixture to the boil, then reduce the heat to a simmer. Cover and cook for 1 hour. Add the capsicum to the casserole, stir it in and cook for another 30 minutes.

To make the topping, mix half of the remaining coriander, the tomato, avocado and the remaining onion. Season and add half of the lime juice.

When the meat is tender, add the remaining coriander and lime juice. Serve with some topping spooned over and a dollop of sour cream.

BEEF SALAD WITH SWEET AND SOUR CUCUMBER

2 LEBANESE (SHORT) CUCUMBERS
6 TEASPOONS CASTER (SUPERFINE) SUGAR
4 TABLESPOONS RED WINE VINEGAR
1 TABLESPOON OIL
300 G (10 OZ) FILLET STEAK, CUT INTO STRIPS
5 SPRING ONIONS (SCALLIONS), CUT INTO PIECES
2 GARLIC CLOVES, CRUSHED
1 TABLESPOON GRATED GINGER
$1^1/_2$ TABLESPOONS SOY SAUCE
4 HANDFULS MIXED LETTUCE LEAVES

Halve the cucumbers lengthways, thinly slice them, then put the slices in a colander. Sprinkle with a little bit of salt and leave for 10 minutes. This will draw out any excess moisture and stop the final flavour from tasting watery. Meanwhile, put 2 teaspoons each of sugar and vinegar in a bowl and stir until the sugar dissolves. Rinse the salt off the cucumber and drain cucumber very thoroughly before dabbing it with a piece of paper towel to soak up any leftover moisture. Combine the cucumber and the vinegar mixture.

Heat the oil in a frying pan until it is smoking – this will only take a minute. Add the steak and fry it for a minute, then add the spring onion and fry for another minute. Add the garlic and ginger, toss everything around once, then add the soy sauce and remaining sugar and vinegar. Let mixture bubble briefly, until the sauce turns sticky.

Put a handful of lettuce leaves on four plates and divide the beef among them. Scatter some cucumber on the beef and serve the rest on the side. Any juices will make a good salad dressing.

MERGUEZ WITH HARISSA AND COUSCOUS

1 TABLESPOON BUTTER
280 G (10 OZ / $1^{1}/_{2}$ CUPS) INSTANT COUSCOUS
4 TABLESPOONS OLIVE OIL
2 TABLESPOONS LEMON JUICE
1 TABLESPOON GRATED LEMON ZEST
1–2 TEASPOONS HARISSA, TO TASTE
2 TABLESPOONS CHOPPED FLAT-LEAF (ITALIAN) PARSLEY
125 G ($4^{1}/_{2}$ OZ) CHARGRILLED RED CAPSICUM (PEPPER), SLICED
4 TABLESPOONS RAISINS
10 MERGUEZ SAUSAGES
GREEK-STYLE YOGHURT

Put the butter in a saucepan with 375 ml (13 fl oz / $1^{1}/_{2}$ cups) water and bring to the boil. Sprinkle in the couscous, stir it into the water, then take it off the stove. Put a lid on the pan and leave it to sit for 5 minutes. Turn on the grill (broiler).

Combine the olive oil and lemon juice and zest. Add harissa to taste and stir together until well mixed. Add the parsley, red capsicum and raisins and leave everything to marinate briefly.

Grill (broil) the sausages for about 8 minutes, turning them often so they brown on all sides.

Meanwhile, take the lid off the couscous, stir it for a minute or two to separate the grains, then stir in the harissa mixture. Serve the couscous with the merguez sliced over it and top with a large dollop of yoghurt.

BEEF COOKED IN GUINNESS WITH CELERIAC PURÉE

2 TABLESPOONS OIL

1.25 KG (2 LB 12 OZ) CHUCK STEAK, CUBED

2 LARGE ONIONS, CHOPPED

2 GARLIC CLOVES, CRUSHED

3 TEASPOONS SOFT BROWN SUGAR

3 TEASPOONS PLAIN (ALL-PURPOSE) FLOUR

185 ML (6 FL OZ/^{3}/$_4$ CUP) GUINNESS OR OTHER DARK BEER

375 ML (13 FL OZ/1^1/$_2$ CUPS) BEEF STOCK

1 BAY LEAF

2 THYME SPRIGS

1 CELERIAC

2 POTATOES, CUBED

315 ML (11 FL OZ/1^1/$_4$ CUPS) MILK

1 TABLESPOON BUTTER

4 SLICES BAGUETTE, TOASTED

1 TEASPOON DIJON MUSTARD

Preheat the oven to 180°(350°/Gas 4). Heat half the oil in a frying pan over high heat and fry the meat in batches until browned all over, adding more oil as you need it. Cook the meat in batches so the temperature stays hot and the meat does not stew. Put the meat in a casserole dish.

Add the onion to the pan and fry it gently over a low heat. When the onion starts to brown, add the garlic and brown sugar and cook until the onion is fairly brown. Stir in the flour, then transfer to the casserole.

Put the Guinness and stock in the frying pan and bring to the boil, then pour the mixture into the casserole (this will collect any meat juices and flavours from the pan). Add the bay leaf and thyme to the casserole and season well. Bring the whole thing to the boil, put a lid on and put the casserole in the oven for 2 hours.

While the casserole is cooking, peel and chop the celeriac. As you chop it, drop the pieces into a bowl of water with a squeeze of lemon juice added; otherwise they will turn brown. Put the potato and celeriac in a saucepan with the milk and bring to the boil. Cover and cook for 15 minutes, or until the celeriac and potato are tender. Mash everything together with the milk. Season well. Add butter.

Spread the baguette with the mustard and serve with the beef ladled over and the celeriac purée on the side.

COOK'S TIP Beef has a rich flavour that lends itself well to many cooking styles, from 3-minute steaks to slow-cooked casseroles, such as this hearty dish. A good source of protein and iron, beef has a wider range of cuts than any other kind of meat. Chuck steak (a relatively inexpensive cut) is perfect for stewing and for other methods of slow cooking, as it turns very tender after a few hours. This is a great dish to do in advance.

STEAK WITH MAÎTRE D'HÔTEL BUTTER

60 G (2¼ OZ) SOFTENED UNSALTED BUTTER
2 TEASPOONS FINELY CHOPPED FLAT-LEAF (ITALIAN) PARSLEY
LEMON JUICE
4 STEAKS, ABOUT 1.5 CM (½ INCH) THICK
1 TABLESPOON OLIVE OIL

Beat the butter to a cream in a small bowl, using a wooden spoon, then beat in a pinch of salt, a pinch of pepper and all the parsley. Add about 1½ teaspoons of lemon juice, a few drops at a time. Leave the butter to harden in the fridge a little, then form into a log shape by rolling it up in greaseproof paper. Refrigerate until you need it.

Season the steaks with salt and pepper on both sides. Heat the oil in a large frying pan and, when it is very hot, add the steaks. Cook them for 2 minutes on each side for rare, 3 minutes on each side for medium, and 4 minutes on each side for well done. The timings may vary depending on the thickness of your steaks – if they are thin, give them a slightly shorter time and if they are thick, cook them for longer.

Cut the butter into slices and put a couple of slices on top of each steak. The heat of the steak will melt the butter. Serve with potatoes and salad or vegetables.

STEAK SANDWICH WITH SALSA VERDE

2 GARLIC CLOVES, CRUSHED

4 HANDFULS FLAT-LEAF (ITALIAN) PARSLEY

2 HANDFULS BASIL LEAVES

2 HANDFULS MINT LEAVES

3 TABLESPOONS OLIVE OIL

2 TEASPOONS CHOPPED CAPERS

2 TEASPOONS LEMON JUICE

2 TEASPOONS RED WINE VINEGAR

4 MINUTE STEAKS

4 CHUNKS CIABATTA OR TURKISH BREAD, HALVED HORIZONTALLY

1 SMALL LEBANESE (SHORT) CUCUMBER, THINLY SLICED

To make the salsa verde, put the garlic and herbs in a food processor with 2 tablespoons of the oil and whizz them together until coarsely chopped. Tip the chopped herbs into a bowl and stir in the capers, lemon juice and vinegar. Season with salt and pepper.

Heat the remaining oil in a frying pan and fry the steaks for a minute on each side – they should cook very quickly and start to brown.

While the steaks are cooking, toast the bread. Spread salsa verde on each of the pieces of bread (be generous) and make the four sandwiches with the steaks and cucumber slices.

LAMB SHANKS WITH CHICKPEAS

1 TABLESPOON OIL
4 LARGE OR 8 SMALL LAMB SHANKS
1 LARGE ONION, FINELY CHOPPED
2 GARLIC CLOVES, CRUSHED
2–3 TEASPOONS HARISSA, TO TASTE
1 CINNAMON STICK
2 x 400 G (14 OZ) TINNED CHOPPED TOMATOES
2 x 300 G (10½ OZ) TINNED CHICKPEAS, DRAINED
16 GREEN OLIVES
1 TEASPOON FINELY CHOPPED PRESERVED LEMON OR LEMON ZEST
2 TABLESPOONS CHOPPED MINT

Heat the oil in a large casserole over medium heat. Fry the lamb shanks until they are well browned all over. Add the onion and garlic and fry for a couple of minutes until the onion starts to soften.

Add the harissa, to taste, cinnamon and salt and pepper to the casserole, stir well, then add the chopped tomato and bring everything to the boil. If there doesn't seem to be enough liquid (the shanks need to be pretty well covered), add some water. Put the lid on and turn the heat down until the liquid is simmering, then cook for 40 minutes.

Add the chickpeas, olives and lemon to the pan and stir them into the liquid. Season to taste and continue cooking with the lid off for another 15–20 minutes. By this time, the lamb should be very tender and almost falling off the bone. If it isn't, keep cooking it, checking every 5 minutes until it is. Using a big spoon, scoop any orange-coloured oil off the top, then stir in the mint. Serve with extra harissa if you would like the sauce to be a little hotter.

LAMB CUTLETS WITH ONION MARMALADE

1 TABLESPOON BUTTER

2 TABLESPOONS OLIVE OIL

2 LARGE ONIONS, FINELY SLICED

2 TEASPOONS SOFT BROWN SUGAR

2 TEASPOONS THYME LEAVES

2 TABLESPOONS FINELY CHOPPED FLAT-LEAF (ITALIAN) PARSLEY

12 FRENCH-TRIMMED LAMB CUTLETS

2 TABLESPOONS LEMON JUICE

Heat the butter and 1 tablespoon of olive oil together in a saucepan. Add the onion, sugar and thyme and stir well. Turn the heat to low, cover the pan and cook the onion, stirring occasionally, for about 20 minutes, or until it is very soft and golden. Season well, stir in the parsley and keep it warm over a very low heat.

Heat the remaining oil in a frying pan or brush a griddle with oil and, when it is hot, add the cutlets in a single layer. Fry for 2 minutes on each side, or until the lamb is browned on the outside but still feels springy when you press it. Add the lemon juice and season well.

Put a small pile of the onion marmalade on each plate and place the cutlets around it. Serve with mashed potato or pumpkin.

HERBED RACK OF LAMB WITH ORANGE SWEET POTATO MASH

2 TABLESPOONS FINELY CHOPPED FLAT-LEAF (ITALIAN) PARSLEY
2 TEASPOONS FINELY CHOPPED THYME
2 TEASPOONS GRATED LEMON ZEST
2 TABLESPOONS DIJON MUSTARD
2 X 8-CUTLET RACK, FRENCH-TRIMMED LAMB, EXCESS FAT REMOVED
2 TABLESPOONS OLIVE OIL
850 G (1 LB 14 OZ) ORANGE SWEET POTATO, PEELED AND CUBED
40 G (1 1/2 OZ) BUTTER
1/2 TEASPOON GROUND CUMIN

Preheat the oven to 220°C (425°F/Gas 7). Put the herbs and lemon zest in a small bowl with the mustard, add plenty of salt and pepper and mix well. Firmly press the herb mixture onto the outside (skinned side) of the rack. Leave the sides and bone side of the rack clean. Put the rack in a roasting tin, herbed side up.

Drizzle the olive oil over the lamb racks and put them in the oven on the top shelf. Roast the lamb for 20 minutes if you like your lamb rare. If you like it cooked to medium, cook it for a further 5 minutes. If you like your lamb cooked right through, give it another 10 minutes.

By now, the herb crust should be browned. When the lamb is cooked, take the racks out of the oven, cover each with a piece of foil and leave to rest for 5 minutes – this allows the juices to soak back into the meat.

To make the mash, put the orange sweet potato in a large saucepan of water and bring it to the boil. Turn the heat down and gently simmer for 10 minutes, or until the sweet potato is tender. Drain. Put the saucepan back on the heat and add butter and cumin. Let the cumin sizzle for a minute, add the sweet potato and again remove the pan from the heat.

Use a potato masher to mash the sweet potato until it is smooth. Season well with salt and pepper.

Carve lamb into separate cutlets, cutting between the bones. Put a pile of orange sweet potato mash on each plate and top with the cutlets.

COOK'S TIP Lamb is traditionally a festival food, and there is certainly something special about bringing a beautifully cooked rack of lamb to the table. Being a slightly fatty meat, it is good paired with an acidic ingredient such as lemon, or with herbs with a robust flavour, such as rosemary or thyme. Sweet root vegetables, such as orange sweet potato mash, also team well with lamb's rich, oily flavour. Make the mash while the lamb is cooking and both should be ready at roughly the same time.

LAMB CURRY

1 KG (2 LB 4 OZ) LEG OR SHOULDER LAMB, CUBED

4 TABLESPOONS PLAIN YOGHURT

2 ONIONS, CHOPPED

1 GREEN CHILLI, ROUGHLY CHOPPED

2 GARLIC CLOVES, CRUSHED

2.5 CM (1 INCH) PIECE GINGER, GRATED

4 TABLESPOONS UNSALTED CASHEW NUTS

2–3 TABLESPOONS KORMA CURRY PASTE, TO TASTE

2 TABLESPOONS OIL

Put the lamb in a bowl with 2 tablespoons of the yoghurt and combine until all the meat cubes are coated.

Put the onion with the chilli, garlic, ginger, cashew nuts and curry paste in a blender, add 2 tablespoons of water and process to a smooth paste. If you don't have a blender, finely chop everything and then add water.

Heat the oil in a large casserole dish over medium heat. Add the blended mixture, season with salt and cook over a low heat for 1 minute, or until the liquid evaporates and the sauce thickens. Add the lamb and slowly bring everything to the boil. Cover the casserole tightly and simmer for 1 hour. Add the remaining yoghurt and continue cooking for a further 30 minutes, or until the meat is very tender. Stir occasionally to stop the meat from sticking to the pan. The sauce should be quite thick. Serve with steamed rice.

SPICED LAMB CUTLET

A FEW DROPS TABASCO SAUCE
1 TEASPOON GROUND TURMERIC
$1/2$ TEASPOON GARAM MASALA
2 GARLIC CLOVES, CRUSHED
2 TABLESPOONS GREEK-STYLE YOGHURT
LEMON JUICE
16 LAMB CUTLETS, FAT TRIMMED OFF

Combine the Tabasco, turmeric, garam masala, garlic and yoghurt to form a paste, adding a few drops of lemon juice. Rub the paste over the cutlets, then put them on a plate, cover them and place in the fridge for about 2 hours. This will allow the flavours to blend and the yoghurt to tenderize the meat.

Turn the grill (broiler) to its highest setting. Sprinkle the chops with salt on both sides, put them on the wire rack and grill (broil) them for about 3 minutes on each side, or until they are brown and sizzling. Squeeze a little more lemon juice over them when cooked. Serve with couscous.

SHEPHERD'S PIE

1 TABLESPOON OIL

1 ONION, FINELY CHOPPED

1 CARROT, FINELY CHOPPED

750 G (1 LB 10 OZ) MINCED (GROUND) LAMB

PLAIN (ALL-PURPOSE) FLOUR

2 TABLESPOONS TOMATO SAUCE (KETCHUP)

1 BEEF STOCK (BOUILLON) CUBE

A FEW DROPS WORCESTERSHIRE SAUCE

6 POTATOES, CUT INTO CHUNKS

4 TABLESPOONS MILK

BUTTER

Preheat the oven to 200°C (400°F/Gas 6). Heat the oil in a frying pan, add the onion and carrot and fry them until they begin to brown around the edges. Add the meat and cook, turning it over every now and then, and mashing out any large lumps with the back of a fork.

When the meat is browned all over, stir in about 2 teaspoons of flour. Add the tomato sauce and sprinkle on the stock cube. Then add 250 ml (9 fl oz/1 cup) water and stir to combine the mixture. Bring to the boil, turn down the heat and simmer gently for about 20 minutes. Season with salt, pepper and some worcestershire sauce.

While the meat is cooking, cook the potato in simmering water until the potato chunks are tender (this will take about 12 minutes). When they are soft, drain well and mash with the milk and plenty of seasoning.

Pour meat into an ovenproof dish or four individual dishes and dollop the potato on top. Dot some butter over the potato and bake (put the baking tray under the dish to catch any drips) for 20 minutes, by which time the top of the potato should be lightly browned. Serve with peas.

PORK CHOPS WITH APPLES AND CIDER

1 TABLESPOON OIL

1 ONION, SLICED

2 GOLDEN DELICIOUS APPLES, CORED AND CUT INTO WEDGES

2 TEASPOONS CASTER (SUPERFINE) SUGAR

2 TEASPOONS BUTTER

4 THICK PORK CHOPS, SNIPPED AROUND THE EDGES TO PREVENT CURLING

4 TABLESPOONS CIDER

4 TABLESPOONS THICK (DOUBLE/HEAVY) CREAM

Heat the oil in a frying pan, add the onion and fry for 5 minutes, or until just softened and beginning to brown. Tip the onion onto a plate.

Add the apple wedges to the pan and fry them for a minute or two – they should not break up, but should start to soften and brown. Add the sugar and butter and shake everything around in the pan until the apples start to caramelize. Add the apples to the onion.

Put the pork chops in the frying pan, add a little seasoning and fry them for 4 minutes on each side, or until cooked through. Put the onion and apple back into the pan and heat through. Add the cider and bring to a simmer. Once the liquid is bubbling, add the cream and shake the pan so that everything is combined. Let the mixture bubble for a minute or two, then season well. Serve with potatoes and a green salad – watercress, with its peppery taste, goes particularly well.

SWEET-AND-SOUR PORK

600 G (1 LB 5 OZ) PORK LOIN, CUBED
1 EGG, LIGHTLY BEATEN
3 TABLESPOONS CORNFLOUR (CORNSTARCH)
3 TABLESPOONS OIL
1 ONION, CUBED
1 RED CAPSICUM (PEPPER), CUBED
2 SPRING ONIONS (SCALLIONS), CUT INTO SHORT LENGTHS
125 ML (4 FL OZ/$\frac{1}{2}$ CUP) CLEAR RICE VINEGAR OR WHITE VINEGAR
2 TABLESPOONS TOMATO SAUCE (KETCHUP)
110 G (4 OZ/$\frac{1}{2}$ CUP) SUGAR

Put the pork cubes and egg in a bowl with 2 tablespoons of the cornflour. Stir everything around to coat the pork well, then tip everything into a sieve and shake off any excess cornflour.

Heat a wok over high heat, add 1 tablespoon of the oil and heat until it just starts to smoke. Add the onion and cook for 1 minute. Add the capsicum and spring onion and cook for a further minute. Add the rice vinegar, tomato sauce and sugar. Reduce the heat and stir everything together until the sugar dissolves (if it hasn't dissolved, the mixture will feel gritty as you stir). Bring to the boil and simmer for about 3 minutes.

Mix the remaining cornflour with 1 tablespoon water and add it to the sweet-and-sour mixture. Simmer for 1 minute, or until the sauce thickens a little. Pour the sauce into a bowl.

Heat the remaining 2 tablespoons of the oil in a non-stick frying pan over a medium heat. As soon as the oil is hot, slide the pork into the pan and cook until browned and crisp. Add the sauce and reheat everything until the sauce is bubbling.

PORK LOIN WITH PICKLED EGGPLANT

2 x 500 g (1 lb 2 oz) piece pork loin fillet (each about 10 cm/
  4 inches long)
1 tablespoon hoisin sauce
1/4 teaspoon five-spice powder
3 tablespoons oil
1 eggplant (aubergine), cut into wedges
1 1/2 tablespoons soy sauce
1 teaspoon sesame oil
1 1/2 tablespoons balsamic vinegar
1/2 teaspoon caster (superfine) sugar
2 bok choy (pak choy), cut into quarters

Put the pork in a dish and add the hoisin sauce, five-spice powder and a
tablespoon of oil. Rub the mixture over the pork fillets and set aside.

Heat another tablespoon of oil in a non-stick frying pan and add the
eggplant. Fry it until it softens and starts to brown, then add the soy
sauce, sesame oil, vinegar and sugar and toss everything together for
about a minute. Tip the eggplant out onto a plate. Wipe out the pan.

Put the last tablespoon of oil in the frying pan and place over a medium
heat. Add the pork fillets and fry them on all sides until they are browned
and cooked through. The time this takes will depend on how thick your
piece of pork is – when it is cooked, it will feel firm when pressed. Put the
eggplant back in the pan to heat through.

Take out the pork and leave it to sit for a minute or two. Cook the bok
choy in a saucepan with a little boiling water for 1 minute, then drain
well. Slice the pork into medallions and serve with the pickled eggplant
and the bok choy.

ROAST PORK WITH CRACKLING

1.5 KG (3 LB 5 OZ) JOINT OF PORK ON THE BONE
3 THYME SPRIGS
6 GARLIC CLOVES
8 BABY ONIONS
4 POTATOES, CUT INTO QUARTERS
2 TABLESPOONS OLIVE OIL
2 GRANNY SMITH APPLES, PEELED AND CHOPPED
2 TEASPOONS CASTER (SUPERFINE) SUGAR
KNOB OF BUTTER
1 TABLESPOON PLAIN (ALL-PURPOSE) FLOUR
250 ML (9 FL OZ / 1 CUP) CHICKEN STOCK

Preheat the oven to 200°C (400°F/Gas 6). Put the joint of pork on a chopping board and remove the layer of skin in one piece by peeling it off. Trim off all but a thin layer of fat from the joint – don't trim it all away or your joint will be horribly dry when you eat it. Score lines into the skin using a very sharp kitchen knife, then rub some salt thoroughly into the skin. Put the skin back on the top of the joint, tucking the thyme in between the skin and fat.

Put the joint with the bone side down in a roasting tin, along with the garlic, onions and potatoes. Drizzle the vegetables with the oil and make sure all the potatoes are coated. Roast the joint for 1 hour 20 minutes, then check whether it is cooked. To do this, push a skewer into the meat, leaving it for 5 seconds, then pull it out and carefully feel how hot it is. If it is very hot, the meat will be cooked. If not, continue cooking and check every 10 minutes.

While the meat is cooking, cook the apple with the sugar and butter and 1 tablespoon of water until it turns into a purée. Mash the apple with the back of a spoon if necessary.

When the meat is cooked, take it out, cover with foil and leave to rest for 10 minutes. Take the potatoes, garlic and onions out of the tin. Spoon off the fat and put the tin over a low heat. Add the flour and stir it in. Cook, stirring constantly for 1 minute. Add stock and let it bubble for 1 minute until it thickens – this will make a thin gravy from the meat juices.

Loosen the chine bone from the joint by running the point of a knife around it. Carve off meat slices, leaving rib bones attached to some and cutting between the bones for others.

COOK'S TIP To make a good roast pork with crackling, you will need a reasonably large piece of meat – so invite some friends to share this with you. Make sure you buy a joint that is easy to carve. Cook some simple vegetables such as carrots or broccoli to go with it.

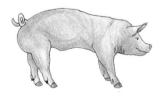

BRAISED SAUSAGES WITH PUY LENTILS

1 TABLESPOON OLIVE OIL
100 G (4 OZ) PANCETTA, CUBED
1 LARGE RED ONION, FINELY CHOPPED
12 TOULOUSE SAUSAGES (OR OTHER GOOD QUALITY PORK SAUSAGES)
2 GARLIC CLOVES, CRUSHED
2 THYME SPRIGS, LEAVES PICKED
270 G (9$\frac{1}{2}$ OZ/1$\frac{1}{3}$ CUPS) PUY LENTILS
750 ML (26 FL OZ/3 CUPS) TINNED CHICKEN CONSOMMÉ OR
   CHICKEN STOCK
200 G (7 OZ) BABY SPINACH LEAVES, FINELY CHOPPED
4 TABLESPOONS CRÈME FRAÎCHE OR SOUR CREAM

Heat the oil in a wide heavy-based frying pan (one with a lid) and fry the pancetta until browned. Take it out, using a slotted spoon, and put it in a bowl. Put the onion in the pan and cook until soft and lightly browned. Remove the onion, using a slotted spoon, and add it to the pancetta. Fry the sausages in the same pan until brown. Return the pancetta and onion to the pan with the sausages.

Add the garlic and the thyme leaves to the frying pan, along with the lentils, and mix everything together. Add the consommé and bring it to the boil. Put a lid on the frying pan and slowly simmer the mixture for 25 minutes. Stir the spinach through.

Season lentils with salt and pepper and stir in the crème fraîche. Serve the sausages and lentils with crusty bread.

SALSICCE WITH WHITE BEANS AND GREMOLATA

3 TABLESPOONS OLIVE OIL

10 SALSICCE (ITALIAN PORK SAUSAGES), CUT INTO CHUNKS

4 GARLIC CLOVES, CRUSHED

6 PIECES CHARGRILLED RED OR YELLOW CAPSICUM (PEPPER)

2 x 400 G (14 OZ) TINNED CANNELLINI BEANS, DRAINED AND RINSED

1 TABLESPOON GRATED LEMON ZEST

3 TABLESPOONS CHOPPED FLAT-LEAF (ITALIAN) PARSLEY

1 TABLESPOON LEMON JUICE

EXTRA VIRGIN OLIVE OIL, FOR DRIZZLING

Heat the olive oil in a frying pan and cook the salsicce until they are browned all over and cooked through. Lift them out of the frying pan with a slotted spoon and set aside.

Put 2 garlic cloves in the frying pan and cook them over gentle heat until they are very soft. Cut the capsicum into strips and add to the pan, along with the beans and salsicce. Stir everything together and cook over gentle heat for 2 minutes just to heat the salsicce through. Season well with salt and pepper.

To make the gremolata, use a mortar and pestle to grind the remaining garlic cloves with a little salt to a paste. Mix in the lemon zest and the chopped parsley and season with salt and pepper.

Just before serving, stir the gremolata through the beans and then finish the dish with a sprinkling of lemon juice and a drizzle of olive oil.

BACON AND AVOCADO SALAD

6 BACON SLICES, RINDS CUT OFF
200 G (7 OZ) GREEN BEANS, TOPPED, TAILED AND HALVED
200 G (7 OZ) BABY SPINACH LEAVES
2 FRENCH SHALLOTS, FINELY SLICED
1 LARGE AVOCADO
PINCH OF SOFT BROWN SUGAR
1 GARLIC CLOVE, CRUSHED
2 TABLESPOONS OLIVE OIL
1/2 TABLESPOON BALSAMIC VINEGAR
1 TEASPOON SESAME OIL

Turn on the grill (broiler). Put the bacon on a tray and grill (broil) it on both sides until it is crisp. Leave it to cool and then break it into pieces.

Bring a saucepan of water to the boil and cook the beans for 4 minutes. Drain them and then hold them under cold running water for a few seconds to cool them down and stop them from cooking any further.

Put the spinach in a large bowl and add the beans, bacon and shallot. Halve the avocado, then cut into cubes and add to the salad.

Combine brown sugar and garlic in a small bowl. Add the rest of the ingredients and whisk together to make a dressing. Pour dressing over the salad and toss well to combine. Grind black pepper over the top and sprinkle with salt.

BEST CHICKEN SANDWICH EVER

2 BONELESS, SKINLESS CHICKEN BREASTS, CUT IN HALF HORIZONTALLY

1 TABLESPOON OLIVE OIL

2 TABLESPOONS LEMON JUICE

4 LARGE PIECES CIABATTA OR TURKISH BREAD, CUT IN HALF
   HORIZONTALLY

2 GARLIC CLOVES, CUT IN HALF

MAYONNAISE

1 AVOCADO, SLICED

2 TOMATOES, SLICED

1 BIG HANDFUL ROCKET (ARUGULA) LEAVES, LONG STEMS SNAPPED OFF

Flatten out each piece of chicken by hitting it either with the flat side of a knife blade or cleaver, or with a meat mallet. Don't break the flesh, just thin it out a little. Trim off any fat or sinew.

Heat oil in a frying pan, add the chicken pieces and fry them on both sides for a couple of minutes, or until they turn brown and are cooked through (you can check by cutting into the middle of one). Sprinkle with lemon juice, then take the chicken out of the pan. Add the bread to the pan, cut side down, and cook for 1 minute, pressing down on it to flatten it and help soak up any juices. You will need to do this in batches.

Take the bread out of the pan, rub the cut side of the garlic over the surface, then spread all the pieces with a generous amount of mayonnaise. Put a piece of chicken on four of the pieces, season and then layer with the avocado and tomato, seasoning as you go. Finish with the rocket and the tops of the bread, then serve.

ROAST CHICKEN WITH GARLIC AND POTATOES

1 LARGE CHICKEN
20 G (^{3}/$_4$ OZ) BUTTER, SOFTENED
1 LEMON, CUT IN HALF
1 ONION, THICKLY SLICED
12 SMALL ALL-PURPOSE POTATOES, CUT IN HALF
12 GARLIC CLOVES, UNPEELED
6 THYME SPRIGS
2 TABLESPOONS OLIVE OIL
250 ML (9 FL OZ/1 CUP) CHICKEN STOCK

Preheat the oven to 200°C (400°F/Gas 6). Rinse chicken in cold water. Trim off any excess fat (around the neck opening). Cut off the parson's nose. Once the skin is loose, push the butter under the skin and press down to spread it around.

Squeeze one lemon half over the chicken, then push it into the cavity of the chicken with a couple of onion slices. Tie the legs together. Put the rest of the onion in a roasting tin and sit the chicken on top. Scatter the potatoes, garlic and thyme around the chicken and drizzle with the oil. Season well. Put the chicken in the oven and roast for 1 hour. Check it to make sure it isn't getting too brown – if it is, cover it with a piece of foil.

After 1 hour, pull one leg of the chicken away from the body. If the juices that run out are clear, the chicken is cooked. If the juices are still pink, keep cooking for another 15 minutes, then check again. Take the chicken out of the tin and put the potatoes back in on their own for 20 minutes. Keep the chicken warm under a piece of foil and a tea towel (dish towel).

Put the chicken on a plate and squeeze the remaining lemon half over it. Pile the potatoes and garlic around it. Put the roasting tin on the stovetop over low heat and add the stock. Boil, stirring, then strain into a jug.

ROAST CHICKEN PIECES WITH HERBED CHEESE

125 G (4 OZ/$\frac{1}{2}$ CUP) HERBED CREAM CHEESE
2 TEASPOONS LEMON ZEST
4 WHOLE CHICKEN LEGS OR BREASTS, SKIN ON
2 LEEKS, CUT INTO CHUNKS
2 PARSNIPS, CUT INTO CHUNKS
2 TEASPOONS OLIVE OIL

Preheat the oven to 200°C (400°F/Gas 6). Mix the cream cheese with the lemon zest. Loosen the skin from the whole legs or chicken breasts and spread a little cream cheese between the skin and flesh on each. Press the skin back down and season it.

Bring a saucepan of water to the boil and cook the leek and parsnip for 4 minutes. Drain them and put them in a baking dish. Drizzle with oil and season well. Place the chicken on top and put the dish in the oven.

Roast for 40 minutes. The chicken skin should be browned and the cheese should have mostly melted to form a sauce over the vegetables. Use a knife to check if the vegetables are cooked and tender. If they are not, remove the chicken and keep warm under foil. Cover baking dish with foil and cook the vegetables for a further 5 minutes.

STIR-FRIED CHICKEN WITH GINGER AND CASHEWS

1 TABLESPOON OIL

6 SPRING ONIONS (SCALLIONS), CUT INTO PIECES

4 GARLIC CLOVES, CRUSHED

6 CM (2½ INCH) PIECE GINGER, FINELY SHREDDED

2 BONELESS, SKINLESS CHICKEN BREASTS, CUT INTO STRIPS

1 LARGE RED CAPSICUM (PEPPER), CUT INTO STRIPS

16 SNOW PEAS (MANGETOUTS)

1 BIG HANDFUL CASHEWS

2 TABLESPOONS SOY SAUCE

2 TEASPOONS SESAME OIL

Heat the oil in a wok until it is smoking – this will only take a few seconds. Add the spring onion, garlic and ginger and stir them around for a few seconds. Next, add the chicken and stir it around until it has all turned white. Add the capsicum and keep stirring. Throw in the snow peas and cashews and stir-fry for another minute or so.

Once the capsicum has started to soften a little, add the soy sauce and sesame oil, toss everything together and tip the stir-fry out into a serving dish. Serve with rice or noodles and more soy sauce on the side.

GRILLED CHICKEN WITH CAPSICUM COUSCOUS

280 G (10 OZ/1½ CUPS) INSTANT COUSCOUS

1 TABLESPOON OLIVE OIL

1 ONION, FINELY CHOPPED

2 ZUCCHINI (COURGETTES), SLICED

4 PIECES OF RED OR YELLOW CHARGRILLED CAPSICUM (PEPPER), CHOPPED

8 SEMI-DRIED (SUN-BLUSHED) TOMATOES, CHOPPED

1 TABLESPOON GRATED ORANGE ZEST

185 ML (6 FL OZ/¾ CUP) ORANGE JUICE

1 LARGE HANDFUL CHOPPED MINT

8 CHICKEN THIGHS OR 4 BREASTS, SKIN ON

30 G (1 OZ) SOFTENED BUTTER

Heat the grill (broiler). Bring 375 ml (13 fl oz/1½ cups) water to the boil in a saucepan, throw in the couscous, then take the pan off the heat and leave it to stand for 10 minutes.

Heat the oil in a frying pan and fry the onion and zucchini until lightly browned. Add the capsicum and semi-dried tomatoes, then stir in the couscous. Stir in the orange zest, 60 ml (2 fl oz/¼ cup) of the orange juice and the mint.

Put the chicken in a small shallow baking dish and dot it with the butter. Sprinkle with the remaining orange juice and season well with salt and pepper. Grill (broil) the chicken for 8–10 minutes, turning it over halfway through. The skin should be browned and crisp.

Serve the chicken on the couscous with any juices poured over.

GREEN CHICKEN CURRY

250 ML (9 FL OZ/1 CUP) COCONUT CREAM

2–3 TABLESPOONS GREEN CURRY PASTE

8 SKINLESS CHICKEN THIGHS OR 4 BREASTS, CUT INTO PIECES

250 ML (9 FL OZ/1 CUP) COCONUT MILK

4 THAI OR 1/2 PURPLE EGGPLANT (AUBERGINE), CUT INTO CHUNKS

2 TABLESPOONS PALM SUGAR (JAGGERY) OR BROWN SUGAR

2 TABLESPOONS FISH SAUCE

4 MAKRUT (KAFFIR LIME) LEAVES, TORN

1 HANDFUL THAI BASIL

1 LARGE RED CHILLI, SLICED

COCONUT MILK OR CREAM, FOR DRIZZLING

Put a wok over low heat, add the coconut cream and let it come to the boil. Stir it for a while until the oil separates out. Don't let it burn.

Add the green curry paste, to taste, stir for 1 minute, then add the chicken. Cook the chicken until it turns opaque, then add the coconut milk and eggplant. Cook for about 10 minutes, or until the eggplant is tender. Add the sugar, fish sauce, lime leaves and half of the basil, then mix everything together.

Garnish with the rest of the basil, the chilli and a drizzle of coconut milk or cream. Serve with rice.

CHICKEN CASSEROLE WITH OLIVES AND TOMATOES

1 TABLESPOON OLIVE OIL

1 ONION, CHOPPED

2 GARLIC CLOVES, CRUSHED

8 PIECES CHICKEN, SKIN ON

1 TABLESPOON TOMATO PASTE (CONCENTRATED PURÉE)

125 ML (4 FL OZ/½ CUP) WHITE WINE

A PINCH SUGAR

6 LARGE RIPE TOMATOES, CHOPPED

3 TABLESPOONS FLAT-LEAF (ITALIAN) PARSLEY, CHOPPED

16 GREEN BEANS, TOPPED, TAILED AND HALVED

ABOUT 16 OLIVES

Heat the oil in a flameproof casserole dish and fry the onion for a minute or two. Add the garlic and the chicken and fry for as long as it takes to brown the chicken all over.

Add the tomato paste, white wine and the sugar, and stir everything together. Add the chopped tomatoes and their juices, the parsley and beans and bring everything to the boil. Turn down the heat, season well and simmer for 30 minutes.

Add the olives and simmer for another 5 minutes. The sauce should be thick by now and the chicken fully cooked. Add more salt and pepper, if necessary. Serve with potatoes, pasta or rice.

FROM THE STREAM & OCEAN

FISH 60

SHELLFISH 66

GRILLED TROUT WITH LEMON BUTTER AND COUSCOUS

185 G (6½ OZ / 1 CUP) INSTANT COUSCOUS
1 TABLESPOON OLIVE OIL
1 ONION, FINELY CHOPPED
4 PIECES OF RED OR YELLOW CHARGRILLED CAPSICUM (PEPPER), CHOPPED
1 HANDFUL PINE NUTS
LEMON JUICE AND ZEST FROM 1 LARGE LEMON
1 HANDFUL CHOPPED MINT
4 RAINBOW TROUT FILLETS, SKIN REMOVED
1 TABLESPOON SOFTENED BUTTER

Heat the grill (broiler). Bring 250 ml (9 fl oz / 1 cup) water to the boil in a saucepan and throw in the couscous. Take the pan off the heat, cover and leave to stand for 10 minutes.

Heat the oil in a frying pan and fry the onion until it is lightly browned. Add the capsicum and pine nuts, then stir in the couscous. Stir through half of the lemon juice and zest, along with the mint.

Put the trout fillets on an oiled baking tray. Mix the butter with the rest of the lemon zest and spread it on the fish. Grill (broil) the fish for about 6 minutes, or until it is just cooked through. Sprinkle on the rest of the lemon juice and season well.

Serve the trout (take it off the tray carefully as it hasn't got any skin to help hold it together) on the couscous with any juices poured over.

SALADE NIÇOISE

600 G (1 LB 5 OZ) SALAD POTATOES

16 SMALL GREEN BEANS, TOPPED, TAILED AND HALVED

4 TABLESPOONS OLIVE OIL

400 G (14 OZ) TUNA STEAK, CUBED

1 GARLIC CLOVE, CRUSHED

1/2 TEASPOON DIJON MUSTARD

1 TABLESPOON WHITE WINE VINEGAR

2 LARGE HANDFULS GREEN LETTUCE LEAVES

12 CHERRY TOMATOES, HALVED

12 BLACK OLIVES

2 TABLESPOONS CAPERS, DRAINED

3 HARD-BOILED EGGS, CUT INTO QUARTERS

4 ANCHOVIES, HALVED

LEMON WEDGES

Cook the potatoes in boiling salted water for 10 minutes, or until tender. Drain them, cut them into wedges, then put them in a bowl. Cook the beans in boiling salted water for 3 minutes, then drain and place under cold running water for a minute. Add them to the potatoes.

Heat a tablespoon of olive oil in a frying pan and, when it is hot, cook the tuna for about 3 minutes, or until the cubes are browned on all sides. Then add them to the potatoes and beans.

Whisk together the garlic, mustard and vinegar. Add the remaining oil in a steady stream, whisking until smooth. Season well.

Cover the base of a bowl with the lettuce leaves. Put the potatoes, beans, tuna, tomatoes, olives and capers on top, and drizzle with the dressing. Decorate with the sliced egg and the anchovies. Serve with lemon wedges.

SAFFRON FISH CAKES WITH HERB CRÈME FRAÎCHE

170 ML ($5^1/_2$ FL OZ/$^2/_3$ CUP) MILK

A PINCH SAFFRON THREADS

500 G (1 LB 2 OZ) WHITE FISH FILLETS

4 LARGE POTATOES, CUT INTO CHUNKS

2 GARLIC CLOVES, UNPEELED

2 TABLESPOONS PLAIN (ALL-PURPOSE) FLOUR

1 TABLESPOON GRATED LEMON ZEST

1 HANDFUL FINELY CHOPPED FLAT-LEAF (ITALIAN) PARSLEY

2 TABLESPOONS THICK (DOUBLE/HEAVY) CREAM

8 TABLESPOONS CRÈME FRAÎCHE OR SOUR CREAM

2 TABLESPOONS FINELY CHOPPED MINT

2 TABLESPOONS FINELY CHOPPED PARSLEY, EXTRA

1 TABLESPOON BUTTER

Put the milk and saffron in a frying pan and heat until simmering. Add the fish, turn up the heat a little and cook until the fish turns opaque and flaky – you might need to turn it over halfway through. Lift the fish out of the milk and into a bowl and break it up with a fork. Keep the milk.

Cook the potato and garlic cloves in simmering water for 12 minutes, or until the potato is tender. Drain the potato and return it to the saucepan. Peel the garlic and add it to the potato, mash everything together and strain in the saffron milk. Mash until smooth, then stir in the fish, flour, half of the lemon zest, the parsley and cream. Season well.

Make the mixture into eight even-sized cakes. Put them in the fridge to chill while you make the herb crème fraîche. To do this, combine the crème fraîche, remaining lemon zest and herbs. Heat the butter in a non-stick frying pan and cook the fish cakes for about 3 minutes on each side, or until heated all the way through. Serve with the herb crème fraîche.

SALMON NORI ROLL WITH SESAME NOODLES

300 G (10½ OZ) PACKET SOBA NOODLES
2 TEASPOONS SESAME OIL
2 TABLESPOONS SESAME SEEDS
2 PIECES SALMON FILLET, ABOUT 10 X 15 CM (4 X 6 INCHES) EACH,
    BONES REMOVED
2 SHEETS NORI
30 G (1 OZ) BUTTER
180 G (6 OZ) BABY SPINACH LEAVES

Cook the noodles in a large saucepan of boiling salted water for about
5 minutes, or until they are just cooked, stirring once or twice to make
sure they are not stuck together. The cooking time will vary depending
on the brand of noodles. Drain the noodles, add sesame oil and a little
salt and pepper, then toss them so they are coated in the oil. Dry-fry the
sesame seeds in a frying pan until they start to colour and smell toasted,
then add them to the noodles. Cover and keep warm.

Cut the salmon fillets in half horizontally and neaten the edges. Cut each
sheet of nori in half with a pair of scissors and lay a piece of salmon fillet
on top of each half. Season well, then roll up the fillets to make neat log
shapes. Trim off any bits of nori or salmon that stick out. Using a sharp
knife, cut each roll into three pieces.

Heat the butter in a non-stick frying pan and fry the pieces of roll until
golden on each side and almost cooked all the way through. This will take
about 4 minutes on each side. Lift out the salmon. Add the spinach to the
pan, stir it around until it wilts, then turn off the heat.

Serve the salmon with the noodles and some spinach on the side.

BASIC PAN-FRIED FISH

2–3 TABLESPOONS PLAIN (ALL-PURPOSE) FLOUR
4 FIRM WHITE FISH CUTLETS
OLIVE OIL, FOR SHALLOW-FRYING

Sift the flour together with a little salt and freshly ground black pepper onto a plate. Pat the fish dry with paper towels, then coat both sides of the cutlets with seasoned flour, shaking off any excess.

Heat about 3 mm (1/8 inch) oil in a large frying pan until very hot. Cook the fish in the hot oil for 3 minutes on one side, then turn and cook the other side for 2 minutes, or until the coating is crisp and well browned. Reduce the heat to low and cook for a further 2–3 minutes, or until the flesh flakes easily when tested with a fork.

Remove the fish from the pan and drain briefly on crumpled paper towels. If you are cooking in batches, keep fish warm while cooking the remaining cutlets. Serve immediately with a salad or steamed vegetables.

HOT AND SOUR FISH STEW

SPICE PASTE

2 LEMON GRASS STEMS, WHITE PART ONLY, EACH CUT INTO THREE PIECES

1 TEASPOON GROUND TURMERIC

SMALL KNOB OF FRESH GALANGAL OR GINGER

3 SMALL RED CHILLIES

1 LARGE GARLIC CLOVE

4 RED ASIAN SHALLOTS

1 TEASPOON SHRIMP PASTE

3 TABLESPOONS OIL

$^1/_2$ SMALL RED CAPSICUM (PEPPER), THINLY SLICED

3 TABLESPOONS TAMARIND PURÉE OR LEMON JUICE

1 TABLESPOON FISH SAUCE

2 TEASPOONS GRATED PALM SUGAR (JAGGERY) OR SOFT BROWN SUGAR

225 G (8 OZ) TINNED SLICED BAMBOO SHOOTS, DRAINED

500 G (1 LB 2 OZ) SKINLESS LEMON SOLE, PLAICE FILLETS OR OTHER FIRM
   WHITE FISH, CUT INTO BITE-SIZED PIECES

2 TABLESPOONS CHOPPED CORIANDER (CILANTRO) LEAVES

1 TABLESPOON CHOPPED MINT

To make the spice paste, put all the ingredients in a food processor and process to a paste. Alternatively, finely chop them and mix by hand.

Heat the oil in a large saucepan, then add the paste. Cook for 10 minutes, stirring. Add the strips of capsicum and cook for a further minute. Pour in 750 ml (26 fl oz/3 cups) water, the tamarind, fish sauce, grated palm sugar and $^1/_2$ teaspoon salt and bring to the boil.

Reduce the heat to low and simmer for 5 minutes, then add the bamboo shoots and fish pieces and poach the fish gently for 3–4 minutes, or until opaque. Stir in the coriander and mint and serve with plenty of rice.

GOAN PRAWN CURRY

1 TABLESPOON OIL
1 TABLESPOON VINDALOO CURRY PASTE
1 SMALL ONION, FINELY CHOPPED
2 TOMATOES, CHOPPED
2 GARLIC CLOVES, CHOPPED
1 GREEN CHILLI, SEEDED AND FINELY CHOPPED
2 CM ($^3/_4$ INCH) PIECE GINGER, GRATED
1 TABLESPOON TAMARIND PURÉE
4 TABLESPOONS COCONUT CREAM
16 RAW PRAWNS (SHRIMP), PEELED AND DEVEINED

Heat oil in a deep frying pan and fry the curry paste for about 1 minute, by which time it should start to release its aromas. Add the onion and fry until it is golden. Add the tomato, garlic, green chilli and ginger and fry over low heat, stirring occasionally, for about 10 minutes, or until the oil separates out from the sauce.

Add the tamarind to the pan and bring everything to the boil. Add the coconut cream and stir. Season with salt.

Add the prawns and bring everything slowly to the boil. (The sauce is not very liquid, but it needs to be made very hot in order to cook the prawns.) Simmer the prawns for 3 minutes, or until they turn bright pink all over. Stir them around as they cook. Serve with Indian breads or rice.

PRAWNS WITH GARLIC AND CHILLI

4 TABLESPOONS OLIVE OIL

4 GARLIC CLOVES, CRUSHED

1 SMALL RED ONION, FINELY CHOPPED

2 DRIED CHILLIES, CUT IN HALF, SEEDS REMOVED

20 RAW LARGE PRAWNS (SHRIMP), PEELED AND DEVEINED, TAILS LEFT ON

2 TOMATOES, FINELY CHOPPED

1 HANDFUL CHOPPED FLAT-LEAF (ITALIAN) PARSLEY OR CORIANDER
(CILANTRO) LEAVES

Heat the oil in a large frying pan or shallow casserole, preferably one that
will look attractive on the table. Add the garlic, onion, chilli pieces and
prawns and cook for about 4 minutes, by which time the prawns should
be pink all over.

When the prawns are cooked, add the tomato and cook for a minute
or two. Season with salt and stir the herbs through. Take the pan to the
table, remembering to put it on a heatproof mat. Serve with bread to
mop up the juices.

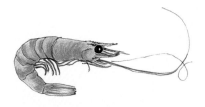

PRAWN AND SNOW PEA STIR-FRY

$1^1/_2$ TABLESPOONS OIL

3 GARLIC CLOVES, THINLY SLICED

1 LEMON GRASS STEM, WHITE PART ONLY, FINELY CHOPPED

$1^1/_2$ TABLESPOONS THINLY SLICED FRESH GINGER

1 KG (2 LB 4 OZ) RAW MEDIUM PRAWNS (SHRIMP), PEELED AND DEVEINED, TAILS INTACT

200 G (7 OZ) SNOW PEAS (MANGETOUTS), TRIMMED AND SLICED INTO 3–4 STRIPS LENGTHWAYS

6 SPRING ONIONS (SCALLIONS), THINLY SLICED ON THE DIAGONAL

80 G ($2^3/_4$ OZ) SNOW PEA (MANGETOUT) SPROUTS

1 TABLESPOON CHINESE RICE WINE

1 TABLESPOON OYSTER SAUCE

1 TABLESPOON SOY SAUCE

Heat a wok to very hot, add the oil and swirl to coat the side. Add the garlic, lemon grass and ginger and stir-fry for 1–2 minutes, or until fragrant. Add the prawns and cook for 2–3 minutes, or until pink and cooked through.

Add the snow peas, spring onion, sprouts, rice wine, oyster and soy sauces and toss until heated through and the vegetables start to wilt. Serves 4–6

SEAFOOD RISOTTO

1.75 LITRES (60 FL OZ/7 CUPS) FISH STOCK
2 TABLESPOONS OLIVE OIL
2 ONIONS, FINELY CHOPPED
2 GARLIC CLOVES, FINELY CHOPPED
1 CELERY STALK, FINELY CHOPPED
440 G (15½ OZ/2 CUPS) RISOTTO RICE
8–10 BLACK MUSSELS, CLEANED AND 'BEARDS' REMOVED
150 G (5½ OZ) SKINLESS BLUE-EYE OR COD FILLET, CUT INTO
   BITE-SIZED PIECES
8 RAW LARGE PRAWNS (SHRIMP), PEELED AND DEVEINED, TAILS INTACT
2 TABLESPOONS CHOPPED FLAT-LEAF (ITALIAN) PARSLEY
2 TABLESPOONS CHOPPED OREGANO

Bring the stock to the boil in a pan. Reduce until simmering, then cover.
Heat the oil in a large saucepan over medium heat. Add the onion, garlic
and celery and cook for 2–3 minutes. Add 2 tablespoons water, cover and
cook for 5 minutes, or until the vegetables soften. Add the rice and cook,
stirring, for 3–4 minutes, or until the rice grains are well coated.

Add 125 ml (4 fl oz/½ cup) of the hot stock to the rice, stirring over low
heat with a wooden spoon until all the stock has been absorbed. Repeat,
adding 125 ml (4 fl oz/½ cup) stock each time until only a small amount
of stock is left and the rice is just tender – this should take 20–25 minutes.

Meanwhile, bring 3 tablespoons water to the boil in a saucepan. Add the
mussels, cover and cook for 4–5 minutes, shaking the pan occasionally,
until the mussels have opened. Discard any unopened mussels. Set aside.

Stir the fish, prawns and remaining stock into the rice and cook for about
7 minutes, or until the seafood is cooked. Add the mussels, cover and take
off the heat for 5 minutes. Stir in the herbs. Rest before serving.

FROM THE KITCHEN GARDEN

POTATOES 72

MIXED VEGETABLES 76

SALAD GREENS 81

MUSHROOMS 84

TOMATOES 86

FRUIT 88

CHIVE GNOCCHI WITH BLUE CHEESE

650 G (1 LB 7 OZ) BOILING (FLOURY) POTATOES
ABOUT 150 G (5$\frac{1}{2}$ OZ) PLAIN (ALL-PURPOSE) FLOUR
2 TABLESPOONS CHOPPED CHIVES
100 G (3$\frac{1}{2}$ OZ) BLUE CHEESE
160 ML (5$\frac{1}{4}$ FL OZ) THICK (DOUBLE/HEAVY) CREAM

Peel the potatoes and cut them into even-sized pieces. Cook them in simmering water for 20 minutes, or until tender. Drain them very well, then mash them in a large bowl. Add three-quarters of the flour, and the chives, along with some seasoning, and combine everything well.

Add enough of the remaining flour to make a mixture that is soft but not sticky. Divide the mixture into four and roll each bit into a sausage shape about 2 cm ($\frac{3}{4}$ inch) across. Cut off lengths about 1.5 cm ($\frac{1}{2}$ inch) long. You don't need to shape the gnocchi more than this.

Bring a saucepan of water to the boil and cook the gnocchi in batches. As the pieces rise to the surface (they will do this when they're cooked through), scoop them out with a slotted spoon and drain well.

While the gnocchi are cooking, put the blue cheese and cream in a pan and heat gently. Put the gnocchi in a large bowl and pour cheese sauce over the top. Gently fold the sauce through the gnocchi and serve.

INDIVIDUAL POTATO GRATINS

1 TABLESPOON OIL

2 ONIONS, FINELY SLICED

2 GARLIC CLOVES, CRUSHED

4 LARGE OR 8 SMALL ALL-PURPOSE POTATOES

120 G (4 OZ/1 CUP) GRATED GRUYÈRE CHEESE

1–2 PINCHES GROUND NUTMEG

170 ML (5^1/$_2$ FL OZ/^{2}/$_3$ CUP) MILK

170 ML (5^1/$_2$ FL OZ/^{2}/$_3$ CUP) THICK (DOUBLE/HEAVY) CREAM

Preheat the oven to 170°C (325°F/Gas 3). Heat the oil in a large frying pan over low heat and add the onion. Stir to coat the onions in oil, then leave to cook until completely soft and translucent but not brown. Stir the onions occasionally to stop them browning in patches. Add the garlic and cook for 1 minute, then turn off the heat.

Thinly slice the potatoes using a sharp knife, making the slices even so they cook at the same rate. Butter four small ovenproof dishes. Equally dividing the ingredients, layer the potato, onion and garlic, grated cheese and nutmeg in the dishes, seasoning as you go. Finish with a layer of potatoes and some cheese. Combine the milk and cream and divide it among the dishes.

Cover the dishes with foil and bake for 10 minutes, then remove the foil and bake for a further 40 minutes, or until the potatoes are completely cooked. Test by pushing a sharp knife through the layers to see if the potato still feels hard. If it does, continue cooking. Leave it to stand for a few minutes before serving so the sauce soaks into the potatoes.

ROAST BABY POTATOES WITH SWEET CHILLI DIP

16–24 BABY POTATOES (DEPENDING ON SIZE)
2 TABLESPOONS OLIVE OIL
2 TEASPOONS FRESH THYME LEAVES
2 TEASPOONS COARSE SALT
4 TABLESPOONS SWEET CHILLI SAUCE
4 TABLESPOONS SOUR CREAM
2 SPRING ONIONS (SCALLIONS), FINELY CHOPPED

Preheat the oven to 200°C (400°F/Gas 6). If any of your potatoes are too big to eat in more than two bites, cut them in half. Put them in a roasting tin with the oil, thyme and salt and mix them around so they are thoroughly coated. Roast for 30–40 minutes, or until cooked through.

Combine the sweet chilli sauce, sour cream and spring onion and serve with the potatoes for dipping.

BAKED POTATOES WITH ROCKET, BROAD BEANS AND BLUE CHEESE

4 LARGE POTATOES
COARSE SALT
200 G (7 OZ) BROAD BEANS
4 TABLESPOONS THICK (DOUBLE/HEAVY) CREAM
60 G (2 OZ) CRUMBLED BLUE CHEESE
4 HANDFULS CHOPPED ROCKET (ARUGULA)

Preheat the oven to 200°C (400°F/Gas 6). Wash the potatoes and, while they are still damp, rub them with a little salt. Prick them several times and then put them in the oven, setting them directly on the oven shelf. Bake for 1 hour, then squeeze gently – they should be soft. If they're still hard, give them another 15 minutes or so.

Cook the broad beans in boiling water for 3 minutes, then drain them well. Peel off the outer grey skins (this is not essential but improves the appearance of the finished dish).

When the potatoes are cooked, cut a small cross in one side of each and squeeze the potatoes around the middle until they open up.

Put the cream in small saucepan, add the broad beans and cook gently for a minute or two, then add the blue cheese and rocket. Stir everything together and when the rocket has wilted, spoon the mixture over the potatoes. Season with black pepper.

SPICED EGGPLANT

    1 LARGE EGGPLANT (AUBERGINE), SLICED
    1 ONION, FINELY CHOPPED
    2 CM ($^3/_4$ INCH) PIECE GINGER, GRATED
    2 GARLIC CLOVES, CRUSHED
    1 RED CHILLI, FINELY CHOPPED
    400 G (14 OZ) TINNED WHOLE TOMATOES
    OIL, FOR FRYING
    $^1/_2$ TEASPOON GROUND TURMERIC
    $^1/_2$ TEASPOON NIGELLA SEEDS
    1 TEASPOON GARAM MASALA
    1 HANDFUL CHOPPED CORIANDER (CILANTRO)

Put the eggplant slices in a colander, sprinkle them with salt and leave them for 30 minutes. Rinse the slices and squeeze them well to get rid of any excess water, then pat dry with paper towels.

Mix the onion, ginger, garlic and chilli with the tomatoes. If you have a blender or food processor, give them a quick whizz in that, but if not, just finely chop the tomatoes first and stir them all together.

Heat a little oil in a large, deep heavy-based frying pan and, when it is hot, add as many eggplant slices as you can fit in a single layer. Cook over medium heat until they are browned on both sides, then drain them in a sieve to get rid of any excess oil. Cool the rest of the eggplant in batches, using as much oil as you need and draining off the excess.

Heat a tablespoon of oil in the frying pan, add the turmeric, nigella seeds and garam masala and stir for a few seconds, then add the tomato. Cook, stirring for 10 minutes, or until the mixture thickens. Add the cooked eggplant so the slices stay whole, cover the pan and cook gently for about 10 minutes. Season with salt to taste and stir the coriander through.

IMAM BAYILDI

2 EGGPLANTS (AUBERGINE)
5 TABLESPOONS OLIVE OIL
1 LARGE ONION, CHOPPED
2 GARLIC CLOVES, CRUSHED
4 RIPE TOMATOES, CHOPPED
1 TEASPOON GROUND CINNAMON
1 HANDFUL CHOPPED FLAT-LEAF (ITALIAN) PARSLEY
250 ML (9 FL OZ/1 CUP) TOMATO JUICE
THICK PLAIN YOGHURT

Preheat the oven to 200°C (400°F/Gas 6). Cut the eggplants in half lengthways. To hollow out the middle, run a small sharp knife around the edge of the cut half, about 1 cm ($^1/_2$ inch) from the skin – don't go through too far or you will cut through the skin on the bottom. Scoop out the flesh in the middle, to leave the two eggplant shells. Chop the flesh roughly.

Heat 3 tablespoons of the oil in a large frying pan and fry the eggplant flesh, onion and garlic until the onion is soft and cooked through. Add the chopped tomato and any juices and stir everything together. Season with salt and pepper and add the cinnamon. Cook the mixture until it is fairly dry, then stir in the parsley.

Fill the eggplant shells with the mixture and put them in a baking dish. Pour the tomato juice around the eggplants – this will help stop the eggplant drying out as it cooks. Drizzle with the remaining oil.

Bake the eggplant shells for 1 hour, by which time the flesh should be tender and the filling browned on top. Serve with some of the tomato juice spooned over and a dollop of yoghurt on top.

CAULIFLOWER RAREBIT

8 THICK SLICES CIABATTA
2 GARLIC CLOVES
600 G (1 LB 5 OZ) CAULIFLOWER, CUT INTO SMALL FLORETS
90 G (3¼ OZ) GRATED GRUYÈRE CHEESE
90 G (3¼ OZ) GRATED CHEDDAR CHEESE
3 TEASPOONS DIJON MUSTARD
1 EGG, BEATEN
2 TABLESPOONS BEER
3 TABLESPOONS THICK (DOUBLE/HEAVY) CREAM

Turn on the grill (broiler) and toast the ciabatta. Cut the garlic cloves
in half and rub the cut sides over one side of each slice of ciabatta.

Bring a saucepan of water to the boil and cook the cauliflower for about
5 minutes, or until it is tender when you prod it with a knife. Drain well.

Mix the cheeses, mustard, egg, beer and cream together. Put the toast on
a baking tray and arrange some cauliflower on top of each piece. Divide
the cheese mixture among the pieces of toast, making sure you coat all
the cauliflower.

Put the rarebits under the grill and grill (broil) them until they are brown
and bubbling.

VEGETABLES WITH POACHED EGG AND CAMEMBERT

12 BABY ONIONS OR FRENCH SHALLOTS
4 TABLESPOONS OLIVE OIL
2 BUNDLES ASPARAGUS, CUT INTO 4 CM ($1^1/_2$ INCH) PIECES
4 ZUCCHINI (COURGETTES), THICKLY SLICED
1 LARGE EGGPLANT (AUBERGINE), CUBED
8 GARLIC CLOVES
2 TABLESPOONS LEMON JUICE
4 EGGS
200 G (7 OZ) CAMEMBERT, CUBED

Preheat the oven to 200°C (400°F/Gas 6). Peel the baby onions and, if they are a little on the large side, cut a cross into each one, leaving them attached at the root end. Don't leave any root on, just enough to keep the quarters together.

Put the oil in a roasting tin and add the onions, asparagus, zucchini and eggplant, along with the garlic, and toss well. Season with salt and pepper. Put the tin in the oven and roast the vegetables for 20 minutes. Sprinkle on the lemon juice and roast for another 10 minutes, or until cooked.

While everything is still roasting, put a large frying pan full of water over a high heat and bring it to the boil. When the water is bubbling, turn the heat down to a gentle simmer. Crack an egg into a cup and slip the egg gently into the water – it should start to turn opaque almost as soon as it hits the water. Do the same with the other eggs, keeping them separate. Don't worry if the eggs spread out in the water. Turn the heat down as low as you can and leave the eggs for 3 minutes.

Divide vegetables among four ovenproof dishes and top with camembert. Put the dishes back in the oven for a couple of minutes to start the cheese melting. Top each dish with a poached egg and black pepper.

MOROCCAN CARROT SALAD WITH OLIVES AND MINT

$1^1/_2$ TEASPOONS CUMIN SEEDS

$^1/_2$ TEASPOON CORIANDER SEEDS

1 TABLESPOON RED WINE VINEGAR

2 TABLESPOONS OLIVE OIL

1 GARLIC CLOVE, CRUSHED

2 TEASPOONS HARISSA

$^1/_4$ TEASPOON ORANGE FLOWER WATER

600 G (1 LB 4 OZ) BABY CARROTS, TOPS TRIMMED, WELL SCRUBBED

40 G ($1^1/_2$ OZ/$^1/_3$ CUP) LARGE GREEN OLIVES, PITTED AND FINELY SLICED

2 TABLESPOONS SHREDDED MINT LEAVES

30 G (1 OZ/ 1 CUP) PICKED WATERCRESS LEAVES

In a small frying pan, dry-fry the cumin and coriander seeds for about 30 seconds or until fragrant. Cool and then grind in a mortar and pestle or spice grinder. Place into a large mixing bowl with the red wine vinegar, olive oil, garlic, harissa and orange flower water. Whisk to combine.

Blanch the carrots in boiling salted water for 5 minutes, until almost tender. Drain into a colander and allow to sit for a few minutes to dry. While still hot, add to the red wine vinegar dressing, and toss gently to coat. Allow to cool to room temperature, letting the flavours in the dressing permeate the carrots. Add the olives and mint. Season well and toss gently to combine. Serve on the watercress leaves.

SPINACH AND ZUCCHINI FRITTATA

1 TABLESPOON OLIVE OIL
1 RED ONION, THINLY SLICED
2 ZUCCHINI (COURGETTE), SLICED
2 GARLIC CLOVES, CRUSHED
150 G (5½ OZ) BABY SPINACH LEAVES
6 EGGS
2 TABLESPOONS CREAM
80 G (2¾ OZ) GRATED EMMENTHAL CHEESE

Heat the oil in a large frying pan and fry the onion and zucchini over medium heat until the mixture is a pale golden brown. Add the garlic and cook it for 1 minute. Add the spinach and cook until wilted and any excess moisture has evaporated. Shake the pan so you get an even layer of mixture. Turn the heat down to low.

Beat the eggs and cream together and season with salt and pepper. Stir in half of the cheese and pour the mixture over the spinach. Cook the bottom of the frittata for about 5 minutes over low heat, or until the egg is just set. While you are doing this, turn on the grill (broiler). When the bottom of the frittata is set, scatter on the rest of the cheese and put the frying pan under the grill to cook the top.

Turn the frittata out of the frying pan after leaving it to set for a minute. Cut it into quarters to serve.

SPINACH WITH GARLIC AND CHILLI

500 G (1 LB 2 OZ) BABY SPINACH LEAVES
2 TABLESPOONS OLIVE OIL
2 GARLIC CLOVES, CRUSHED
1 RED CHILLI, SEEDED AND FINELY CHOPPED
3 TABLESPOONS POURING CREAM
CAYENNE PEPPER

Wash the spinach thoroughly and shake it dry, leaving a little water clinging to the leaves. If you choose to use a packet of frozen spinach, defrost it thoroughly and drain it very well – squeeze it with your hands to get rid of excess moisture.

Heat the oil in a frying pan, add the garlic and chilli and cook for a few seconds, being careful not to burn them. Add the spinach and stir it through the oil. Put the lid on the pan for a minute to create some steam. Remove the lid and turn up the heat. Stir the spinach, turning it over frequently until all the liquid has evaporated, then season well. Drizzle with the cream and dust with cayenne pepper.

SPINACH SALAD WITH CHICKEN AND SESAME DRESSING

300 G (10½ OZ) BABY SPINACH LEAVES

1 LEBANESE (SHORT) CUCUMBER, PEELED AND DICED

3 SPRING ONIONS (SCALLIONS), SHREDDED

1 CARROT, CUT INTO MATCHSTICKS

2 BONELESS, SKINLESS CHICKEN BREASTS, COOKED

2 TABLESPOONS TAHINI

2 TABLESPOONS LIME JUICE

3 TEASPOONS SESAME OIL

½ TEASPOON SUGAR

1 SMALL PINCH CHILLI FLAKES

2 TABLESPOONS SESAME SEEDS

1 SMALL HANDFUL CORIANDER (CILANTRO) LEAVES

Put the spinach in a large bowl. Scatter the cucumber, spring onion and carrot over the top.

Shred the chicken breasts into long pieces and scatter over the vegetables.

Combine the tahini, lime juice, sesame oil, sugar and chilli flakes, then add salt to taste. Drizzle this dressing over the salad.

Cook sesame seeds in a dry frying pan over low heat for a minute or two, stirring them around. When they start to brown (take care not to burn them) and smell toasted, tip them over the salad. Scatter the coriander leaves over the top. Toss the salad just before serving.

MUSHROOM SOUP

2 TABLESPOONS BUTTER
1 ONION, FINELY CHOPPED
1 KG (2 LB 4 OZ) FIELD MUSHROOMS, ABOUT 9 LARGE, FINELY CHOPPED
2 GARLIC CLOVES, CRUSHED
2 TABLESPOONS DRY SHERRY
750 ML (26 FL OZ/3 CUPS) CHICKEN OR VEGETABLE STOCK
2 TABLESPOONS FINELY CHOPPED FLAT-LEAF (ITALIAN) PARSLEY
THICK (DOUBLE/HEAVY) CREAM

Melt the butter in a saucepan and fry the onion until it is translucent but not brown. Add the mushrooms and garlic and continue frying. Initially, the mushrooms may give off a lot of liquid, so keep frying until it is all absorbed back into the mixture. This will take 10–12 minutes.

Add the sherry to the pan, turn up the heat and let the mixture bubble – this burns off the alcohol but leaves the flavour. Cool slightly, then transfer to a blender. Whizz together until a smooth paste forms, then add the stock and blend until smooth. Add the parsley and a couple of tablespoons of cream and blend again. Pour the mixture back into the saucepan and heat gently. Serve with plenty of fresh, crusty bread.

GRILLED MUSHROOMS WITH GARLIC AND CHILLI

4 LARGE OR 8 MEDIUM FIELD MUSHROOMS
2 TABLESPOONS SOFTENED BUTTER
2 GARLIC CLOVES, CRUSHED
1 SMALL RED CHILLI, SEEDED AND FINELY CHOPPED
3 TABLESPOONS FINELY CHOPPED FLAT-LEAF (ITALIAN) PARSLEY
4 THICK SLICES CIABATTA
TOMATO CHUTNEY OR RELISH
CRÈME FRAÎCHE

Put the grill (broiler) on and cover the grill rack with a piece of foil so any juices stay with the mushrooms as they cook. Gently pull the stalks out of the mushrooms and wipe or peel the skins if they are dirty.

Combine the butter, garlic, chilli and parsley and spread some over the inside of each mushroom. Make sure the butter is quite soft so it spreads easily. Season well.

Grill (broil) the mushrooms under medium heat for about 8 minutes – they need to be cooked right through. Test the centres with the point of a knife if you are not sure.

Toast the bread, spread some tomato chutney or relish on each slice, then stop with a mushroom (or two) and serve straight away. A dollop of crème fraîche will make the whole dish even more decadent.

TOMATO AND PESTO BRUSCHETTA

8 THICK SLICES CIABATTA
3 TABLESPOONS OLIVE OIL
6 TABLESPOONS READY-MADE PESTO
8 RIPE ROMA (PLUM) TOMATOES
4 TABLESPOONS MASCARPONE CHEESE

Turn the grill (broiler) to its highest setting. Brush both sides of each piece of bread lightly with olive oil and put the bread on a baking tray. Grill (broil) for 3 minutes on each side, or until crisp and golden brown.

Spread a little pesto over each piece of bruschetta and take them off the tray. Slice the tomatoes into four pieces lengthways and drain for a minute on a piece of paper towel – this will stop the juice from the tomatoes turning the bruschetta soggy. Put the tomato slices on the baking tray.

Grill the tomatoes for about 5 minutes, by which time they will start to cook and brown at the edges. When cooked, layer four slices onto each piece of bruschetta. Put the bruschetta back on the tray and grill for a further minute to heat through. Add a dollop of mascarpone and a little more pesto to each bruschetta and serve hot.

TOMATO CAPONATA WITH MOZZARELLA

1 EGGPLANT (AUBERGINE), CUBED

OLIVE OIL

1 ONION, CUBED

2 CELERY STALKS, SLICED

1 RED CAPSICUM (PEPPER), CUBED

4 RIPE ROMA (PLUM) TOMATOES, CHOPPED

16 RED AND 16 YELLOW CHERRY TOMATOES, CUT IN HALF

2 TABLESPOONS RED WINE VINEGAR

A PINCH SUGAR

2 TABLESPOONS CAPERS, RINSED

12 BLACK OLIVES, UNPITTED

300 G (10$\frac{1}{2}$ OZ) MOZZARELLA, CHOPPED

1 HANDFUL ROUGHLY CHOPPED FLAT-LEAF (ITALIAN) PARSLEY

Cook the eggplant in boiling salted water for a minute, then drain it. Squeeze out any excess moisture with your hands.

Heat a tablespoon of olive oil in a large frying pan and add the eggplant. Brown on all sides over high heat, adding more oil if you need to. When the eggplant is cooked, take it out and drain it on paper towels.

Add more oil to the pan, reduce the heat and cook the onion and celery for 5 minutes, or until soft. Add the capsicum and cook for 2 minutes. Add chopped tomato and 1 tablespoon of water. Simmer for 5 minutes, or until the mixture is quite dry, then stir in the cherry tomatoes.

Season the mixture with pepper. Add vinegar, sugar, capers and olives and cook everything for 2–3 minutes over a low heat. Add the drained eggplant and cook it for 5 minutes. Take the mixture off the heat and leave it to cool. Toss the mozzarella and parsley through the caponata and serve it with a green salad and some bread to mop up the juices.

MANGO FOOL

2 SMALL VERY RIPE MANGOES
250 ML (9 FL OZ/1 CUP) GREEK-STYLE YOGHURT
4 TABLESPOONS THICK (DOUBLE/HEAVY) CREAM

Take the flesh off each mango. The easiest way to do this is to slice down either side of the stone so you have 2 'cheeks'. Make crisscross cuts through the mango flesh on each cheek, almost through to the skin, then turn each cheek inside out and slice the flesh from the skin into a bowl. Cut the rest of the flesh from the stone.

Purée the flesh either by using a food processor, blender or stick blender, or if you don't have any of these, just mash the flesh thoroughly.

Put a spoonful of mango purée in the bottom of a small glass, bowl or cup and top with a spoonful of yoghurt. Repeat until you have used up all the mango and yoghurt. Spoon the cream over each serving and swirl the layers together just before serving.

SPICED FRUIT SALAD

80 G (2³/₄ OZ/¹/₃ CUP) CASTER (SUPERFINE) SUGAR
3 SLICES GINGER
1 BIRD'S EYE CHILLI, CUT IN HALF AND SEEDED
LIME JUICE AND ZEST FROM 1 LIME
FRUIT (A MIXTURE OF WATERMELON, MELON, MANGO, BANANA, CHERRIES,
    LYCHEES, KIWI FRUIT, OR ANYTHING ELSE YOU FANCY), ENOUGH FOR
    FOUR PORTIONS.

Put the sugar in a saucepan with 80 ml (2¹/₂ fl oz/¹/₃ cup) water and the ginger and chilli. Heat until the sugar melts, then leave to cool before adding the lime juice and zest. Discard the ginger and chilli.

Put the prepared fruit in a bowl and pour the syrup over it. Leave to marinate in the fridge for 30 minutes.

Serve with ice cream or sorbet – coconut ice cream is a good match.

APPLE AND PASSIONFRUIT CRUMBLE

4 PASSIONFRUIT
4 GREEN APPLES
135G (5 OZ/^{2}/$_3$ CUP) CASTER (SUPERFINE) SUGAR
60 G (2^1/$_4$ OZ/1 CUP) SHREDDED COCONUT
90 G (3^1/$_4$ OZ/^{3}/$_4$ CUP) PLAIN (ALL-PURPOSE) FLOUR
80 G (2^3/$_4$ OZ) UNSALTED BUTTER, CHOPPED
THICK (DOUBLE/HEAVY) CREAM OR ICE CREAM, TO SERVE

Preheat the oven to 180°C (350°F/Gas 4). Grease a 1 litre (35 fl oz/4 cup) baking dish. Push the passionfruit pulp through a sieve, discarding the pulp, and place the juice in a bowl. Peel, core and thinly slice the apples and add to the passionfruit juice, along with 50 g (1^3/$_4$ oz/^{1}/$_4$ cup) of the sugar. Mix well, then transfer the mixture to the baking dish.

Combine the remaining sugar, the coconut, flour and butter in a bowl. Use your fingertips to rub the butter into the coconut and flour until the mixture resembles coarse crumbs. Pile evenly over the apple mixture.

Bake the crumble for 25–30 minutes, or until the topping is crisp and golden. Serve warm with cream or ice cream.

ZUPPA INGLESE

4 THICK SLICES SPONGE OR MADEIRA (POUND) CAKE

4 TABLESPOONS KIRSCH

150 G (5½ OZ) RASPBERRIES (FRESH OR DEFROSTED FROM FROZEN)

150 G (5½ OZ) BLACKBERRIES (FRESH OR DEFROSTED FROM FROZEN)

2 TABLESPOONS CASTER (SUPERFINE) SUGAR

250 ML (9 FL OZ/1 CUP) READY-MADE CUSTARD

250 ML (9 FL OZ/1 CUP) CREAM, LIGHTLY WHIPPED

ICING (CONFECTIONERS') SUGAR, FOR DUSTING

Put a piece of sponge cake on each of four deep plates and brush or sprinkle with kirsch. Leave kirsch to soak in for a few minutes.

Put the raspberries and blackberries in a saucepan with the caster sugar. Gently warm through over low heat so that the sugar just melts, then leave the fruit to cool.

Spoon the fruit over the sponge, pour the custard on top and, finally, dollop on the cream and dust with icing sugar.

REAL LEMON PIE

FILLING
4 THIN-SKINNED LEMONS
450 G (1 LB/2 CUPS) CASTER (SUPERFINE) SUGAR
4 EGGS, LIGHTLY BEATEN

310 G (11 OZ/$2^1/_2$ CUPS) PLAIN (ALL-PURPOSE) FLOUR
80 G ($2^3/_4$ OZ/$^1/_3$ CUP) CASTER (SUPERFINE) SUGAR
225 G (8 OZ) COLD UNSALTED BUTTER, CHOPPED
2–3 TABLESPOONS ICED WATER
MILK, FOR BRUSHING
CREAM, TO SERVE

Start making the filling a day ahead. Wash the lemons well, then dry. Peel two lemons, removing all the white pith with a small, sharp knife, then slice the flesh very thinly, removing any seeds. Leave the other two lemons unpeeled and slice very thinly, removing any seeds. Place in a bowl with the sugar and stir until the lemon slices are coated. Cover and leave to stand overnight.

Sift the flour and a pinch of salt into a large bowl, then stir in the sugar. Using your fingertips, lightly rub in the butter until the mixture resembles breadcrumbs. Make a well in the centre and gradually add most of the iced water to the well, mixing with a flat-bladed knife until a rough dough forms, adding a little extra iced water if necessary. Turn out onto a lightly floured work surface, then gently gather the dough together. Divide in half and roll each portion into a 30 cm (12 inch) circle. Cover with plastic wrap and refrigerate for 30 minutes.

Meanwhile, preheat the oven to 180°C (350°F/Gas 4). Lightly grease a 23 cm (9 inch) pie dish that is at least 3 cm ($1^1/_4$ inches) deep. Roll one sheet of pastry around the rolling pin, then lift and ease it into the pie dish, gently pressing to come up the side. Cover all the pastry with plastic wrap and refrigerate for 20 minutes.

Meanwhile, finish preparing the filling. Measure out 750 ml (26 fl oz/ 3 cups) of the lemon slices and liquid. Place in a bowl with the beaten eggs, stirring to mix well. Spoon the mixture into the chilled pastry case, then cover with the pastry circle, trimming the pastry and crimping the edges to seal. Re-roll the pastry scraps and cut out decorative shapes. Place on top of the pie and brush with milk.

Bake for 50–55 minutes, or until the pastry is golden brown. Remove from the oven and allow to cool slightly. Serve straight from the dish, with cream for drizzling over. Real lemon pie is best eaten the day it is made. Serves 8

VARIATION For an apple pie, toss 5 peeled, cored and thinly sliced apples in 3 tablespoons caster (superfine) sugar with a pinch of cinnamon. Fill the pie, cover with a pastry lid and make some slashes in the top. Dust with caster sugar and bake for 50 minutes.

FROM THE DAIRY

EGGS 96

CHEESE 99

MILK, CREAM & BUTTER 104

HUEVOS RANCHEROS

1 TABLESPOON OLIVE OIL
1 LARGE WHITE ONION, FINELY CHOPPED
1 GREEN CAPSICUM (PEPPER), FINELY CHOPPED
2 GARLIC CLOVES, CRUSHED
$1/2$ TEASPOON DRIED OREGANO
2 TOMATOES, CHOPPED
400 G (14 OZ) TINNED CHOPPED TOMATOES
4 EGGS
4 FLOUR TORTILLAS
75 G ($2^1/2$ OZ/$^1/2$ CUP) CRUMBLED FETA

Put the olive oil in a frying pan (one with a lid) over medium heat. Add onion and capsicum and fry gently for 2 minutes, or until soft.

Add the garlic and stir briefly. Add the oregano, fresh and tinned tomatoes and 90 ml (3 fl oz) water. Bring to the boil, then reduce the heat and simmer gently for 5 minutes, or until the sauce thickens. Season with salt and pepper.

Smooth the surface of the mixture. Make four hollows with the back of a spoon. Break an egg into each hollow and put the lid on the pan. Cook the eggs for 5 minutes, or until they are set.

While the eggs are cooking, heat tortillas according to the instructions on the packet and cut each one into quarters. Serve the eggs with some feta crumbled over them and the tortillas on the side.

SPANISH OMELETTE WITH SMOKED SALMON

2 TABLESPOONS OLIVE OIL

400 G (14 OZ) ALL-PURPOSE POTATOES, PEELED AND CUBED

1 LARGE ONION, FINELY CHOPPED

6 EGGS

2 TABLESPOONS CHOPPED DILL

6 SLICES SMOKED SALMON

3 TABLESPOONS MASCARPONE CHEESE

4 HANDFULS MIXED SALAD LEAVES

Heat the oil in a large non-stick frying pan and add the potato cubes. Fry them gently, stirring so they brown on all sides and cook through to the middle. Depending on the size of the potato pieces, this will take about 10 minutes.

When the potato is cooked, add the onion and cook gently until soft and translucent. Turn on the grill (broiler).

When the onion is almost ready, break the eggs into a bowl and whisk them with salt and pepper and the dill.

Shred smoked salmon into pieces and add to the frying pan. Add the mascarpone in little dollops. Using a spatula, pull the mixture into the centre of the pan and level it off. Pour the eggs over the top and cook for 5 minutes, or until just set.

Put the frying pan under the grill for a minute to lightly brown the top of the omelette. Slide the omelette out of the pan. Cut into four wedges. Serve with salad leaves.

FRIED EGG AND RED ONION WRAPS

1 TABLESPOON OLIVE OIL
2 LARGE RED ONIONS, THICKLY SLICED
1 LARGE RED CAPSICUM (PEPPER), SLICED
1 TABLESPOON BALSAMIC VINEGAR
4 EGGS
4 PIECES OF LAVASH BREAD
4 TABLESPOONS SOUR CREAM
SWEET CHILLI SAUCE

Heat the olive oil in a non-stick frying pan. Add the onion. Cook slowly,
stirring occasionally until the onion softens and is translucent. Add the
capsicum and continue cooking until both are soft. Increase the heat and
stir for 1–2 minutes, or until they start to brown. Stir in the vinegar.

Remove the mixture to a side plate. Carefully break eggs into the pan,
keeping them separate if you can. Cook over a gentle heat until just set.

Heat the lavash in a microwave or under a grill (broiler) for a few seconds
(you want them to be soft and warm). Lay the breads out on a board,
spread a tablespoon of sour cream in the centre of each, then drizzle with
a little chilli sauce. Place a heap of the onion and capsicum mixture on
each and top with an egg. Season with salt and pepper.

Fold in one short end of each piece of lavash and then roll each one up
lengthways to contain the filling.

FATTOUSH WITH FRIED HALOUMI

2 SMALL CUCUMBERS

3 PITTA BREADS

2 GARLIC CLOVES, CRUSHED

2 TABLESPOONS LEMON JUICE

5 TABLESPOONS OLIVE OIL

4 SPRING ONIONS (SCALLIONS), SLICED

4 TOMATOES, DICED

1 LARGE GREEN CAPSICUM (PEPPER), DICED

1 LARGE BUNCH FLAT-LEAF (ITALIAN) PARSLEY, CHOPPED

2 TABLESPOONS CHOPPED MINT

2 TABLESPOONS CHOPPED OREGANO

750 G (1 LB 10 OZ) HALOUMI CHEESE, CUT INTO 8 SLICES

SUMAC (OPTIONAL)

Turn on the grill (broiler). Peel the cucumber, cut it into quarters lengthways, then cut each piece into thick slices. Put the slices in a sieve and sprinkle with a little salt to help drain off any excess liquid, which would make the salad soggy.

Split each pitta bread in half and toast on both sides to make the bread crisp. Break bread into small pieces. Mix the garlic, lemon juice and 4 tablespoons of the oil to make a dressing. Rinse and drain cucumber.

Put the cucumber, spring onion, tomato, capsicum and the chopped herbs in a large bowl. Add the dressing and toss everything together well.

Heat the last tablespoon of oil in a large non-stick frying pan and fry the haloumi cheese on both sides until it is browned. Scatter the bread over the salad. Serve the fattoush with the slices of haloumi on top. Sprinkle with a little sumac, if you are using it.

TOASTED CHEESE, AÏOLI AND HAM

1 LOAF CIABATTA OR TURKISH BREAD
1 LARGE GARLIC CLOVE, CRUSHED
6 TABLESPOONS MAYONNAISE
4–6 SLICES HAM
10 CHOPPED SEMI-DRIED TOMATOES
2 TABLESPOONS CAPERS, CHOPPED
6–8 SLICES CHEDDAR CHEESE

Turn on the grill (broiler). Cut the bread in half horizontally and then into four equal pieces. Toast all the pieces. To make the aïoli, mix the garlic into the mayonnaise and season it well with salt and pepper.

Spread the aïoli over the insides of each sandwich. Put a slice of ham on four of the pieces and then divide the semi-dried tomatoes and capers among them. Top with enough cheese slices to make a generous layer. Put them on a baking tray.

Grill (broil) the sandwiches until the cheese melts and starts to bubble and then put the tops back on and press down firmly. Cut each sandwich in half diagonally to serve.

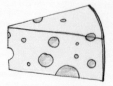

GRILLED NACHOS

2 x 300 G (10 OZ) PACKET CORN CHIPS
4 TOMATOES, CHOPPED
2 RED ONIONS, FINELY CHOPPED
2–3 JALAPEÑO CHILLIES, FINELY SLICED
2 TABLESPOONS LIME JUICE
4 TABLESPOONS CHOPPED CORIANDER (CILANTRO) LEAVES
225 G (8 OZ) FETA CHEESE, CRUMBLED

Turn on the grill (broiler). Arrange the nachos on four ovenproof plates.
(Tin or enamel camping plates work well.)

Scatter the tomato, onion and chilli on top of the nachos, then drizzle
with the lime juice and season with salt. Scatter the coriander and feta
cheese over the top, making sure the nachos are well covered.

Grill (broil) the nachos until they start to brown around the edges and
the cheese starts to melt. Serve hot but take care with the plates – they
will be very hot, too.

TWICE-BAKED CHEESE SOUFFLÉS

- 250 ML (9 FL OZ/1 CUP) MILK
- 3 WHOLE BLACK PEPPERCORNS
- 1 ONION, CUT IN HALF AND STUDDED WITH 2 CLOVES
- 1 BAY LEAF
- 60 G (2¼ OZ) BUTTER
- 60 G (2¼ OZ/½ CUP) SELF-RAISING FLOUR
- 2 EGGS, SEPARATED
- 125 G (4½ OZ/1 CUP) GRATED GRUYÈRE CHEESE
- 250 ML (9 FL OZ/1 CUP) CREAM
- 60 G (2 OZ/ ½ CUP) FINELY GRATED PARMESAN CHEESE

Preheat the oven to 180°C (350°F/Gas 4). Lightly grease four 125 ml (4 fl oz/½ cup) ramekins.

Place the milk, peppercorns, onion and bay leaf in a saucepan and heat until nearly boiling. Remove the saucepan from the heat and let the milk infuse for 10 minutes. Strain, discarding the solids.

Melt the butter in a saucepan over a medium heat, add the flour and cook, stirring, for 1 minute. Stirring constantly, add the milk a little at a time, returning the mixture to a simmer between additions and stirring well to prevent lumps from forming. Simmer the mixture, stirring, until it boils and thickens.

Transfer the mixture to a bowl, add the egg yolks and gruyère cheese and stir to combine well.

Whisk the egg whites with electric beaters until soft peaks form, then gently fold into the cheese sauce. Divide the mixture among the ramekins and place in a baking dish half-filled with hot water. Bake for 15 minutes. Remove from the baking dish, cool and refrigerate until needed.

Preheat the oven to 200°C (400°F/Gas 6), remove the soufflés from the ramekins and place them on ovenproof plates. Pour the cream over the top and sprinkle with parmesan. Bake for 20 minutes, or until puffed and golden. Serve immediately.

COOK'S TIP Soufflés are always impressive but cooking them can make even the most proficient cook a little panicky at times. There seems to be too much involved and no second chances. This twice-baked version, however, is foolproof and allows you to cook the soufflés once and then put them in the fridge overnight. Next day, all you need to do is pour the cream over, add the parmesan and cook them for the second time. Everyone will think you whipped up these delicious morsels at the last minute, whereas you know, in fact, that you made them calmly with no fear of failure.

PAVLOVA

4 EGG WHITES
230 G (8½ OZ/1 CUP) CASTER (SUPERFINE) SUGAR
2 TEASPOONS CORNFLOUR (CORNSTARCH)
1 TEASPOON WHITE VINEGAR
500 ML (17 FL OZ/2 CUPS) THICK (DOUBLE/HEAVY) CREAM
3 PASSIONFRUIT, TO DECORATE
STRAWBERRIES, TO DECORATE

Preheat the oven to 160°C (315°F/Gas 2–3). Line a 32 x 28 cm (13 x 11 inch) baking tray with baking paper.

Place the egg whites and a pinch of salt in a small bowl. Using electric beaters, beat until stiff peaks form. Add the sugar gradually, beating constantly after each addition, until the mixture is thick and glossy and all the sugar has dissolved.

Using a metal spoon, fold in the cornflour and vinegar. Spoon the mixture into a mound on the prepared tray. Lightly flatten the top of the pavlova and smooth the sides. (This pavlova should have a cake shape and be about 2.5 cm (1 inch) high.) Bake for 1 hour, or until the meringue has turned to a pale cream colour and is crisp. Remove from the oven while warm and carefully invert onto a plate. Allow to cool.

Lightly whip the cream until soft peaks form. Spread over the soft centre. Decorate with pulp from the passionfruit and halved strawberries. Cut into wedges to serve.

GREEK SHORTBREAD

200 G (7 OZ) UNSALTED BUTTER, SOFTENED

1 TEASPOON FINELY GRATED ORANGE ZEST

250 G (9 OZ/2 CUPS) ICING (CONFECTIONERS') SUGAR

1 EGG

1 EGG YOLK

310 G (11 OZ/$2^1/_2$ CUPS) PLAIN (ALL-PURPOSE) FLOUR

$1^1/_2$ TEASPOONS BAKING POWDER

1 TEASPOON GROUND CINNAMON

250 G (9 OZ/$1^2/_3$ CUPS) BLANCHED ALMONDS, TOASTED
    AND FINELY CHOPPED

Preheat the oven to 160°C (315°F/Gas 2–3). Line two baking trays with baking paper.

Put the butter and orange zest in a bowl. Sift half the icing sugar into the bowl, then beat using electric beaters until light and fluffy. Add the egg and egg yolk and beat until well combined.

Sift the flour, baking powder and cinnamon into a bowl. Using a metal spoon, gently fold into the butter mixture along with the almonds until well combined.

Roll level tablespoons of the mixture into logs, then form into crescent shapes and place on the baking trays. Bake for 15 minutes, or until lightly golden. Remove from the oven and leave to cool on the trays for about 5 minutes, then transfer to a wire rack to cool.

While the shortbreads are still warm, dredge with the remaining sifted icing sugar. Just before serving, dust heavily again with icing sugar. Greek shortbread will keep for up to 1 week, stored in a cool place in an airtight container, or can be frozen in an airtight container for up to 8 weeks.

BLUEBERRY CHEESECAKE

125 G (4½ OZ) BUTTER
100 G (3½ OZ/1 CUP) ROLLED (PORRIDGE) OATS
100 G (3½ OZ/¾ CUP) WHOLEMEAL BISCUITS (GRAHAM CRACKERS),
    FINELY CRUSHED
2 TABLESPOONS SOFT BROWN SUGAR

FILLING
375 G (13 OZ/1½ CUPS) LIGHT CREAM CHEESE
100 G (3½ OZ/⅓ CUP) RICOTTA CHEESE
90 G (3¼ OZ/⅓ CUP) CASTER (SUPERFINE) SUGAR
125 G (4½ OZ/½ CUP) SOUR CREAM
2 EGGS
1 TABLESPOON FINELY GRATED ORANGE ZEST
1 TABLESPOON PLAIN (ALL-PURPOSE) FLOUR

TOPPING
250 G (9 OZ/1⅔ CUPS) BLUEBERRIES
240 G (8½ OZ/¾ CUP) BLACKBERRY JAM
60 ML (2 FL OZ/¼ CUP) CHERRY BRANDY

Grease a 20 cm (8 inch) spring-form cake tin and line the base with baking paper. Melt the butter in a saucepan, add the oats and biscuit crumbs and mix well. Stir in the sugar. Press half the mixture into the base of the tin in an even layer. Gradually press the remainder around the sides, but not quite all the way up to the rim, using a glass to ease it into place. Refrigerate for 10–15 minutes.

Preheat the oven to 180°C (350°F/Gas 4). To make the filling, beat the cream cheese, ricotta cheese, sugar and sour cream with electric beaters until smooth. Beat in the eggs, orange zest and flour. Put the cake tin on a flat baking tray to catch any drips. Pour the filling into the crust and bake for 40–45 minutes, or until the filling is just set. Remove from the oven and leave in the tin to cool to room temperature.

To make the topping, scatter the blueberries on top of the cheesecake. Push the jam through a sieve into a small saucepan with the cherry brandy. Stir over medium heat until smooth and then simmer for about 2–3 minutes. Carefully brush the mixture over the blueberries. Refrigerate for several hours or overnight, until well chilled. Serves 8.

COOK'S TIP Blackberries, raspberries or strawberries can be used instead of blueberries for the topping – just substitute the same weight in berries. If using strawberries, they need to be quartered or sliced first.

ALMOND CROISSANT PUDDING

4 GOOD-QUALITY, DAY-OLD ALMOND CROISSANTS, TORN INTO
   SMALL PIECES
4 EGGS
90 G (3¼ OZ/HEAPED ⅓ CUP) CASTER (SUPERFINE) SUGAR
250 ML (9 FL OZ/1 CUP) MILK
250 ML (9 FL OZ/1 CUP) THICK (DOUBLE/HEAVY) CREAM
½ TEASPOON FINELY GRATED ORANGE ZEST
80 ML (2½ FL OZ/⅓ CUP) ORANGE JUICE
2 TABLESPOONS FLAKED ALMONDS
ICING (CONFECTIONERS') SUGAR, FOR DUSTING
ICE CREAM OR WHIPPED CREAM, TO SERVE

Preheat the oven to 180°C (350°F/Gas 4). Grease the base and side of
a 20 cm (8 inch) deep-sided cake tin and line the base with baking paper.
Place the croissant pieces in the tin.

Using electric beaters, beat the eggs and sugar together until thick and
pale. Combine the milk and cream in a saucepan and bring almost to
the boil. Gradually pour the milk mixture over the egg mixture, stirring
constantly. Add the orange zest and juice and stir well. Slowly pour the
mixture over the croissants, allowing the liquid to be completely absorbed
before adding any more. Sprinkle over the flaked almonds, then bake for
45 minutes, or until cooked when tested with a skewer.

Cool the pudding in the tin for 10 minutes, then invert onto a serving
plate. Cut the pudding into wedges, dust with icing sugar and serve warm
with cream or ice cream. Serves 6

BANANA AND BLUEBERRY PANCAKES

250 ML (9 FL OZ/1 CUP) BUTTERMILK

1 EGG, LIGHTLY BEATEN

1 TABLESPOON MELTED BUTTER

1 TEASPOON NATURAL VANILLA EXTRACT

115 G (4 OZ) PLAIN (ALL-PURPOSE) FLOUR

1 TEASPOON BAKING POWDER

2 RIPE BANANAS, MASHED

100 G (3½ OZ/⅔ CUP) BLUEBERRIES

1 TEASPOON VEGETABLE OIL

MAPLE SYRUP, TO SERVE

Preheat the oven to 120°C (235°F/Gas ½). Combine the buttermilk, egg, butter and vanilla in a bowl and whisk to mix well. Sift in the flour, baking powder and ½ teaspoon salt, then quickly stir until just combined, taking care not to over mix; the batter should be a little lumpy. Stir in the bananas and blueberries.

Heat the oil in a frying pan over medium heat. Working in batches, add 60 ml (2 fl oz/¼ cup) of batter to the pan for each pancake, then cook for 3 minutes, or until the bases of the pancakes are golden brown. Turn over and cook for a further minute, or until risen slightly and cooked through. Place cooked pancakes on a plate, cover with aluminium foil and keep warm in the oven while cooking the remaining pancakes. Serve the hot pancakes drizzled with maple syrup. Makes about 12

INDEX

A

almond croissant pudding 108
apple and passionfruit crumble 90

B

bacon and avocado salad 50
banana and blueberry pancakes 109
beef
  beef cooked in Guinness with
    celeriac purée 32
  beef salad with sweet and sour
    cucumber 30
  chunky chilli con carne 29
  hamburgers with fresh corn relish 28
  rice noodles with beef and black beans 17
  steak with maître d'hôtel butter 34
  steak sandwich with salsa verde 35
blueberry cheesecake 106
bruschetta, tomato and pesto 86
butternut and feta risotto 22

C

cauliflower rarebit 78
cheese
  blueberry cheesecake 106
  cauliflower rarebit 78
  attoush with fried haloumi 99
  grilled nachos 101
  roast chicken pieces with herbed cheese 53
  toasted cheese, aïoli and ham 100
  tomato caponata with mozzarella 87
  twice-baked cheese soufflés 102
chicken
  best chicken sandwich ever 51
  chicken casserole with olives and
    tomatoes 57
  green chicken curry 56
  grilled chicken with capsicum couscous 55
  pulao with fried onions and spiced
    chicken 24
  roast chicken with garlic and potatoes 52
  roast chicken pieces with herbed cheese 53
  spinach salad with chicken and sesame
    dressing 83
  stir-fried chicken with ginger and
    cashews 54
  Thai-style chicken with glass noodles 18
chilli con carne, chunky 29
chive gnocchi with blue cheese 72

curry
  Goan prawn curry 66
  green chicken curry 56
  amb curry 40

D

desserts
  almond croissant pudding 108
  apple and passionfruit crumble 90
  banana and blueberry pancakes 109
  blueberry cheesecake 106
  mango fool 88
  pavlova 104
  real lemon pie 92
  spiced fruit salad 89
  zuppa inglese 91

E

eggplant
  imam bayildi 77
  pork loin with pickled eggplant 45
  spiced eggplant 76
eggs
eggs continued
  fried egg and red onion wraps 98
  huevos rancheros 96
  Spanish omelette with smoked salmon 97
  vegetables with poached egg and
    camembert 79

F

fattoush with fried haloumi 99
fish
  basic pan-fried fish 64
  grilled trout with lemon butter and
    couscous 60
  hot and sour fish stew 65
  saffron fish cakes with herb crème fraîche 62
  salade Niçoise 61
  salmon kedgeree 20
  salmon nori roll with sesame noodles 63
  Spanish omelette with smoked salmon 97

G

Goan prawn curry 66
Greek shortbread 105

H

ham

ham continued

ham, artichoke and spinach lasagne 12
toasted cheese, aïoli and ham 100
hamburgers with fresh corn relish 28
hot and sour fish stew 65
huevos rancheros 96

I

imam bayildi 77

L

lamb
herbed rack of lamb with orange sweet
potato mash 38
lamb continued
lamb curry 40
lamb cutlets with onion marmalade 37
lamb shanks with chickpeas 36
shepherd's pie 42
spiced lamb cutlet 41
lemon pie, real 92
loaf, soy and linseed 15

M

mains
basic pan-fried fish 64
beef cooked in Guinness with celeriac
purée 32
braised sausages with puy lentils 48
butternut and feta risotto 22
chicken casserole with olives and
tomatoes 57
chunky chilli con carne 29
Goan prawn curry 66
green chicken curry 56
grilled chicken with capsicum
couscous 55
grilled trout with lemon butter and
couscous 60
ham, artichoke and spinach lasagne 12
herbed rack of lamb with orange sweet
potato mash 38
hot and sour fish stew 65
lamb curry 40
lamb cutlets with onion marmalade 37
lamb shanks with chickpeas 36
merguez with harissa and couscous 31
pork chops with apples and cider 43
pork loin with pickled eggplant 45
prawns and snow pea stir-fry 68
pulao with fried onions and spiced
chicken 24
rice noodles with beef and black beans 17

mains continued

roast chicken with garlic and potatoes 52
roast chicken pieces with herbed cheese 53
roast pork with crackling 46
saffron fish cakes with herb crème
fraîche 62
salmon kedgeree 20
salmon nori roll with sesame noodles 63
salsicce with white beans and
gremolata 49
seafood risotto 69
shepherd's pie 42
spaghetti carbonara 9
spaghetti puttanesca 8
Spanish omelette with smoked
salmon 97
special fried rice with prawns 21
spiced lamb cutlet 41
spinach and ricotta ravioli 10
steak with maître d'hôtel butter 34
stir-fried chicken with ginger and
cashews 54
sweet-and-sour pork 44
Thai-style chicken with glass noodles 18
mango fool 88
merguez with harissa and couscous 31
minestrone with pesto 11
Moroccan carrot salad with olives and
mint 80
mushrooms
grilled mushrooms with garlic and chilli 85
mushroom soup 84

N

nachos, grilled 101

O

onions
fried egg and red onion wraps 98
lamb cutlets with onion marmalade 37
pulao with fried onions and spiced
chicken 24

P

pancakes, banana and blueberry 109
pasta
ham, artichoke and spinach lasagne 12
spaghetti carbonara 9
spaghetti puttanesca 8
spinach and ricotta ravioli 10
pavlova 104
pizza margherita 14
pork
pork chops with apples and cider 43
pork loin with pickled eggplant 45

pork continued
roast pork with crackling 46
weet-and-sour pork 44
potatoes
baked potatoes with rocket, broad beans
and blue cheese 75
chive gnocchi with blue cheese 72
individual potato gratins 73
roast baby potatoes with sweet chilli dip 74
prawns
Goan prawn curry 66
prawns with garlic and chilli 67
prawns and snow pea stir-fry 68
pecial fried rice with prawns 21
pulao with fried onions and spiced
chicken 24

R
ramen noodle soup with char siu 16
rice
pulao with fried onions and spiced
chicken 24
rice noodles with beef and black beans 17
special fried rice with prawns 21
risotto
butternut and feta 22
seafood risotto 69

S
saffron fish cakes with herb crème fraîche 62
salads
bacon and avocado salad 50
beef salad with sweet and sour
cucumber 30
fattoush with fried haloumi 99
Moroccan carrot salad with olives and
mint 80
salade Niçoise 61
spinach salad with chicken and sesame
dressing 83
salmon
salmon kedgeree 20
salmon nori roll with sesame noodles 63
Spanish omelette with smoked salmon 97
salsicce with white beans and gremolata 49
sandwiches
best chicken sandwich ever 51
fried egg and red onion wraps 98
hamburgers with fresh corn relish 28
steak sandwich with salsa verde 35
toasted cheese, aïoli and ham 100
sausages
braised sausages with puy lentils 48

sausages continued
merguez with harissa and couscous 31
salsicce with white beans and
gremolata 49
seafood risotto 69
seafood see fish; prawns
shepherd's pie 42
shortbread, Greek 105
soufflés, twice-baked cheese 102
soup
minestrone with pesto 11
mushroom soup 84
ramen noodle soup with char siu 16
soy and linseed loaf 15
spaghetti carbonara 9
spaghetti puttanesca 8
Spanish omelette with smoked salmon 97
spiced eggplant 76
spiced fruit salad 89
spiced lamb cutlet 41
spinach with garlic and chilli 82
spinach and ricotta ravioli 10
spinach salad with chicken and sesame
dressing 83
spinach and zucchini frittata 81
steak with maître d'hôtel butter 34
steak sandwich with salsa verde 35
stir-fry, prawns and snow peas 68
sweet-and-sour pork 44

T
Thai-style chicken with glass noodles 18
tomatoes
pizza margherita 14
tomato caponata with mozzarella 87
tomato and pesto bruschetta 86

V
vegetables with poached egg and
camembert 79

Z
zuppa inglese 91